Robert Bell

Report on Explorations on the Churchill and Nelson Rivers and around Gods and Island Lakes

Robert Bell

Report on Explorations on the Churchill and Nelson Rivers and around Gods and Island Lakes

ISBN/EAN: 9783744717779

Printed in Europe, USA, Canada, Australia, Japan

Cover: Foto ©Andreas Hilbeck / pixelio.de

More available books at **www.hansebooks.com**

GEOLOGICAL SURVEY OF CANADA.

ALFRED R. C. SELWYN, F.R.S., F.G.S., Director.

REPORT

ON EXPLORATIONS ON THE

CHURCHILL AND NELSON RIVERS

AND AROUND

GOD'S AND ISLAND LAKES

1879

BY

ROBERT BELL, M.D., F.G.S., C.E.

PUBLISHED BY AUTHORITY OF PARLIAMENT.

Montreal:
DAWSON BROTHERS.

—

1880

GEOLOGICAL SURVEY OFFICE,

MONTREAL, May 4th, 1880.

ALFRED R. C. SELWYN, ESQ., F.R.S., F.G.S.,
Director of the Geological Survey.

SIR,—My report, containing a summary of the results of the operations of the season of 1879, is herewith respectfully submitted.

I have the honour to be,

Sir,

Your obedient servant,

ROBERT BELL.

TABLE OF CONTENTS.

(C)
PAGE

REPORT

ON EXPLORATIONS ON THE

CHURCHILL AND NELSON RIVERS

AND AROUND

GOD'S AND ISLAND LAKES,

1879.

BY

ROBERT BELL, M.D., F.G.S., C.E.

Before proceeding to state the results of the work to which this report refers, I shall give a brief narrative of the season's operations and mention the methods pursued in endeavouring to accomplish the objects we had in view. In 1878 I had made a track-survey and a geological examination of the boat-route from Lake Winnipeg to Hudson's Bay by way of Oxford and Knee lakes, and the rivers thence to York Factory. I had also made topographical and geological surveys of the lower part of Nelson River, and of the upper part of the same stream, from Lake Winnipeg nearly to Split Lake, leaving unfinished the central part. In 1879 I was to complete this and to examine as much of the Churchill River as the season would permit. In order to accomplish this I proceeded, as before, by way of the city of Winnipeg to Norway House, which I again made my headquarters for the season. It is due to the officers of the Hudson's Bay Company that I should here again express our indebtedness to them for their uniform kindness and for the substantial assistance which they often rendered, enabling us to accomplish much more than would otherwise have been possible. In this connection I must mention more particularly Mr. Grahame, the Chief Commissioner, Mr. J. McTavish of Fort Garry, Mr. Wm. Flett of the Stone Fort, Mr. Roderick Ross of Norway House, Mr. C. Sinclair of Oxford House, Mr. Linklater of Island Lake, Mr. J. R. Spencer of Fort Churchill, and Mr. Joseph Fortescue of York Factory.

Methods pursued.

Previous surveys.

Work for 1879.

Acknowledgment of assistance.

Assistant.   I was assisted during the season by Mr. A. S. Cochrane, who had accompanied me on a former survey, and through his efficiency as an explorer the extent of our field-work was largely increased. On my journey west, by way of the lakes, I picked up, at the Sault Ste. Marie,

Men.   three men whose merits I had tested on long explorations in previous years.

A few days after our arrival in Manitoba, the officers of the Hudson's Bay Company kindly allowed myself and party to take passage by the steamer *Colville* (which also towed our York boat) from Lower Fort Garry to George's Island, or the greater part of the distance to

Norway House.   Norway House, for which they made no charge. They also gave me the use of the York boat referred to for the summer.

Before reaching Norway House, although diligent enquiry was made, no reliable information could be obtained with regard to the

Want of information.   Churchill River, the central portion of the Nelson, or the country lying between these two streams; and even at this post very little was known on the subject. This arises from the fact that both these rivers

Abandoned rivers.   have long since been abandoned as " voyaging " routes by the Hudson's Bay Company, and also that no Indians live at or near the parts I was to examine. At Norway House it was ascertained that a route for

Route to Churchill River   small canoes existed between Split Lake on the Nelson and the head-waters of the Little Churchill River, and I determined to follow it and the latter stream to the Great Churchill, and to descend this river to the sea. As it was necessary to find out everything as we went along, the question of how best to finish my survey of the central part of the Nelson River was left to be decided as circumstances might determine.

Mr. Cochrane's instructions.   Before leaving Norway House, Mr. Cochrane was instructed to proceed to God's Lake and Island Lake and to make track-surveys and a geological examination of their shores, as well as of his routes in going from Oxford House and returning to it again. The position of Oxford House I had determined the previous year. Mr. Cochrane performed this service in a very satisfactory manner.

Norway House to Fort Churchill.   I left Norway House on the 16th of July with four Indians and two small canoes, and reached Fort Churchill, by the route above indicated, on the 5th of August, having completed a track-survey and made a geological examination of the whole distance. On reaching the junction of the Little with the Great Churchill River, I left most of my outfit in charge of one man, and with the other three made an upward exploration of the main river for two days, so that the time occupied on the journey between Norway House and the sea, at Fort Churchill, was only seventeen days, two of which were lost owing to rain.

From the mouth of the Churchill I started in a boat with my own men to examine the coast of Hudson's Bay northward, but circumstances soon obliged me to return. The Hudson's Bay Company's ship from London arrived the same day that I returned to the mouth of the river, and the captain kindly agreed to give a passage to myself and men to York Factory. While the ship was lying at Fort Churchill, I made an approximate survey of the surrounding region. *Ship from London.*

At York Factory I obtained some provisions, and, with the men who accompanied me from Norway House, proceeded in the same small canoes to ascend the Nelson River to the point which had been reached when *en route* for Churchill. The river above the first rapids proved very difficult to ascend and the journey occupied a longer time than I had expected, but with the aid of the game and fish which we obtained we managed to subsist. *Ascend the Nelson River.*

A short distance above Split Lake, the Grass River enters the Nelson on the west side. Having already explored the Nelson above this point both in 1878 and 1879, I determined to ascend the Grass River, and from one of its branches I again reached the Nelson at the foot of Sipiwesk Lake. I next made a track-survey of the north-western channels and arms of this lake, and then of the channels to and from Duck Lake, as well as of the latter lake itself. *Grass River. Other surveys.*

In going up from Pipestone Lake to Norway House I surveyed a small channel of the Nelson, which runs for some miles through the eastern part of Ross' Island, of which both sides were mapped in 1878, and the island found to be over fifty miles in length. In the course of these explorations along the Nelson River, observations were taken for latitude, longitude and the variation of the compass, and a number of photographs were obtained. *Channel through Ross' Island. Observations.*

On reaching Norway House again, I found that Mr. Cochrane had returned only a day or two in advance of myself, and as soon as we could get ready we set out for Manitoba in the same York boat in which we had come. The season proving very stormy with headwinds, we were three weeks in reaching Lower Fort Garry. Having made a track-survey in 1878 of the west side of Lake Winnipeg from the Dog's Head southward, the east side was followed on the present occasion from this place to the mouth of Red River, and a sketch of its outline taken. *Return to Manitoba. Sketch of part of East shore of Lake Winnipeg*

When in Manitoba, it was my intention to have made a geological examination of the line of the Canadian Pacific Railway eastward from Red River to Rat Portage, but it was not found practicable to do so, and as the season was well advanced I returned to Montreal, which I reached on the 11th of November. *Return to Montreal.*

The following list shows the respective lengths of the several track-surveys which were made by myself:—

	Miles.
1. Canoe-route from Split Lake to Was-kai-ow-a-ka Lake	42
2. Shores of this lake	30
3. Little Churchill River, following its course	172
4. Great Churchill River, following its course	169
5. Shore lines, &c., in the vicinity of Fort Churchill	40
6. Nelson River, including some re-surveys; but not the lakes on its course	212
7. Shores and connecting channels of Gull, Split, and Sipi-wesk lakes, not including islands and the smaller bays	232
8. Grass River and lakes in its course, counting only the straightest line through each lake, between the points at which I entered and left it	108
9. Part of the east shore of Lake Winnipeg between the Dog's Head and the mouth of Red River	64
Total	1,069

These surveys, checked by the numerous latitudes which were taken, and knowing the longitudes of a few points and the magnetic variation which was frequently ascertained, enable us to lay down, with sufficient accuracy for present purposes, a considerably amount of topography. As, however, it is proposed that I shall continue operations during the coming season in the same field, and also extend the area explored, it is considered best to publish a map of the results of both years' work at the same time. For the same reason I propose next year to describe the whole region more fully, so that the present report may be considered as being to some extent only provisional. The area covered by Mr. Cochrane's explorations having being confined within narrower limits, may be considered as finished, and his map accompanies this report.

The following list shows the number of miles of track-survey accomplished by Mr. Cochrane:—

	Miles.
1. The channels between Great and Little Playgreen Lakes	49
2. Jack River, from Rossville mission to above the second rapids	25
3. Canoe-route from Knee Lake to God's Lake	27
4. Shores of main body of God's Lake	136
5. Canoe-route, including Rat, Clearwater and Touchwood lakes, between Oxford Lake and God's Lake	67
6. Canoe-route between God's and Island lakes	69
7. Shores of Island Lake, all around	213
Total	586

A somewhat less accurate track-survey, embodying upwards of forty

miles of shore-lines, which was made of the upper division of God's
Lake, is not included in the foregoing statement.

The surveys mentioned in the above lists, amounting in the aggregate to 1,655 lineal miles, were completed in less than three months Time and men
with the assistance of only six men. Although they are made only as required.
accessory to our geological work, they afford a good knowledge of the
principal geographical features of the country, and may be found useful for various other purposes at any future time. Besides performing
the foregoing track-surveys, both Mr. Cochrane and I resurveyed in Resurveys.
the same manner considerable stretches, not included in the above
statements, which I had gone over in 1878 for the sake of checking
distances and obtaining greater accuracy of detail.

In the course of the above surveys, I took a large number of observations both of the sun and pole-star, for latitude and the variation of
the compass. Others for longitude were also made at a few points. Astronomical observations.
In addition to this astronomical work, the reading of the barometer
was constantly kept for ascertaining differences of level of water and
the elevations on land, and the temperatures of rivers and lakes were Elevations and
noted as indicated by the thermometer. There was not a very great temperatures.
diversity of scenery. However, I exposed about forty prepared dry
plates, which gave as many photographic views as it was thought Photographs.
worth taking, in order to show the characters of the different parts of
the region explored, or to represent any points of particular interest
met with. A few of these have been used in preparing the illustra- Illustrations.
tions which accompany this report.

I made a considerable collection of plants as I went along, and Prof.
Macoun, of Albert University, Belleville, has kindly furnished a list
of the specimens which I submitted to him. This will be found Botanical
in the appendix. The best part of my collection was made along the collections.
Nelson River, but the greater portion of this was unfortunately lost,
owing to an accident. Professor Macoun has, however, found 237
species among the specimens brought home. Notes were kept in regard to the nature of the woods in all localities visited, and the Distribution of
geographical range of the various shrubs and timber-trees was recorded. trees.
Some remarks on this subject will be found further on. The information derived from a study of the distribution of the trees and shrubs,
and of the flora generally, in any district, affords us one of the most
certain means of judging of its climate for agricultural purposes. It
will be seen that the general trend of the northern limits of the forest- Northern limits
trees in the region under consideration agrees with that of the isother- of species.
mal lines as determined from other data.

The character of the soil was always noted, as well as any facts Soil.

which had been ascertained by the officers of the Hudson's Bay Company or others in regard to the crops which might be raised. Besides our own experience in regard to the nature of the climate, information was collected from others as to rain, snow, frosts, winds, &c., all with a view to ascertain as far as possible how much of the country may some day be turned to account for the support of man. Facts bearing on these subjects will be given in the course of this report.

Climate.

Attention was paid to the zoology of the country explored as far as our time would permit.

Zoology.

Mammals.—I continued to gather information as to the habits and life-history of all the species known to inhabit the district, both by direct observation and by prosecuting my enquiries among the officers of the Hudson's Bay Company and the better class of Indian hunters. I have been collecting notes on this subject for several years from all parts of the basin of Hudson's Bay, and I propose to give the results in a future report. In the meantime I beg to express my obligations to the gentlemen referred to and also to Dr. Elliott Coues, of Washington, D.C., the well-known authority in this department, for the correct determination of some of the smaller species.

Habits of Mammals.

Dr. Elliott Coues.

Birds.—A list will be found in the appendix of fifty-five species of birds, of which I obtained specimens of either the skins or eggs. This list may be of some interest in extending our knowledge of the geographical range and of the breeding grounds of some of the species enumerated. Although the number of birds whose occurrence was noticed is considerable, I have not added their names to this list, in case of doubt. During the coming season I hope to procure specimens of many of them, along with others not hitherto noticed.

List of specimens collected.

Fishes.—In travelling "light" in small canoes I was unable to carry along alcohol for preserving the smaller species, and none can be obtained at the posts in the district. When opportunities occurred, however, I preserved specimens of the larger fishes with common salt. Before publishing a list of the fishes of the district, it will be well to take advantage of the opportunities which it is expected will be afforded during the coming summer for adding to the number of species already known, and increasing our knowledge of the distribution of the others. I may mention that I have ascertained the existence of twenty-one species in Lake Winnipeg or the adjacent waters. From specimens which I sent to Professor Baird, Professor Gill, of the Smithsonian Institution, has determined the herring white-fish, which is caught in abundance at the mouths of the Nelson and Hayes rivers, to be *Coregonus Artedi.* The same fish is abundant at the mouths of all the rivers around James' Bay. The pike-perch from York Factory ho

Fishes of Lake Winnipeg.

Herring white-fish.

Pike-perch.

identifies as *Stizostethium Canadense*. A fine grayling was obtained in Grayling.
the brooks flowing into the Churchill near the sea. From a specimen
submitted to Prof. Gill, he finds the species to be *Thymallus signifer*.
The salmon frequenting the mouth of the Churchill is the same species Salmon.
which is more abundant on the east side of Hudson's Bay, and was
referred to in my report for 1877. A sea-trout is also found in the Sea-trout.
mouths of the Churchill, Nelson and Hayes rivers, as well as along the
east side of Hudson's and James' bays.

Insects.—The Coleoptera, which I collected in the region of the Coleoptera.
Churchill and Nelson rivers, were kindly determined by Dr. J. L.
LeConte, of Philadelphia, and a list of them will be found in the
appendix. The Lepidoptera of the district which I explored last Lepidoptera.
summer have been studied by Herr Geffcken, formerly of Stuttgart,
Germany, who has kindly furnished me with the list of species given
in the appendix. The specimens were collected principally by the
Venerable Archdeacon Kirkby, who resided until 1879 at York
Factory.

Mollusks.—Owing to the muddy and brackish nature of the water, Hudson's Bay.
no mollusks are found in the part of Hudson's Bay near York Factory.
About the mouth of the Churchill river the only living species observed
were the common mussel (*Mytilus edulis*) and a species of *Littorina*.
Dead shells were abundant on the beach, of *Pecten Islandicus, Cardium
Islandicum, Mya arenaria, M. truncata, Astarte lactea* and *Rhynchonella
psittacea*, but all these appear to have been washed out of the drift-clay,
which abounds from below the sea-level upward. A list of the fresh- List of fresh-
water shells collected in the district, together with some from Manitoba, water species.
is given in the appendix.

WATERS OF THE RED AND ASSINIBOINE RIVERS.

In the earlier days of the Geological Survey, analyses were made by
Dr. T. Sterry Hunt of the waters of the great rivers of what then con-
stituted Canada, as well as of those of many mineral springs and wells.
As it was considered desirable to continue this important work in reference to the principal rivers now included in the Dominion, I obtained Samples from
samples of the waters of the Nelson, Red and Assiniboine rivers for large rivers.
experiment. A complete qualitative and quantitative analysis of each
of the two last mentioned is now being made in the laboratory of the
Geological Survey, and the results will be reported on by Mr. Hoffmann. Having also brought home samples of each of these waters Former
six years before, which were afterwards submitted to Dr. Baker samples.
Edwards, F.C.S., for analysis, I shall give his results in referring to
the subject of the water-supply of the city of Winnipeg. The bottles

containing the sample of the Nelson River water were unfortunately broken on the way to Montreal, when our boxes were violently tossed about on a steamer during a gale of wind in Lake Huron.

The Water Supply of the City of Winnipeg.

City of Winnipeg.

Owing to the rapid growth of the city of Winnipeg, which already contains a large population, the question of providing it with a cheaper,

Importance of a better supply.

and, if possible, a better supply of water than that afforded by the present primitive and inadequate method has become a matter of great

Wells.

importance. The waters derived from the wells sunk in the stratified clay in and around the city, although clear and sparkling, are not always pleasant to the taste, and they are evidently too highly charged with mineral salts to be desirable for domestic use. Besides these objections, the quantity which might be obtained from such wells would, no doubt, prove quite inadequate for the wants of a large town.

Waters of the Red and Assiniboine rivers.

The water of either the Red or Assiniboine River is fairly good, and as these streams afford the most convenient sources from which to draw an unlimited supply, any information as to the nature of their respective waters will be of interest at the present time. Dr. Edwards' analyses, to which I have referred, were made in June and July, 1879. The samples were collected by myself on the 18th of October, 1873— that of the Assiniboine at Fort Garry Ferry, and that of Red River a few miles above the confluence of the two rivers. In each case the

Collecting of samples.

samples were taken from the centre of the stream. They were preserved in hard glass bottles, at a pretty uniform temperature, in a cellar in Montreal until required for analysis. Having been kept for such a length of time, a portion of the organic matter has most likely been lost, but the mineral constituents have probably not been affected to any practical extent. Before the analyses were undertaken the greater part of the suspended impurities had settled to the bottom, and the decanted water, being almost clear, was not filtered. The quantities operated upon were smaller than would have been desirable, but owing

Dr. Baker Edwards' analyses.

to Dr. Edwards' skill, and his experience as a water analyst, I have no doubt his figures represent very nearly the composition of the respective rivers at the above date. The samples handed to Messrs. Hoffmann and Adams, and which were collected in the corresponding period in the month of October (1879), were taken from each river at a short

Probable change in composition.

distance above its junction with the other. It may be expected that some change has taken place in the composition of these waters in the interval of six years, owing to various causes, among which may be mentioned the dredging by the United States authorities of the bottom of the Red River throughout a considerable part of its course, to the

cultivation and drainage of land, and perhaps also to the increased rain-
fall in Manitoba during the last few years. These analyses may,
therefore, be found to possess some historical interest:—

WATER OF THE ASSINIBOINE IN 1873.

	Total solid contents in grains per Imperial gallon.	
1. Organic matter (loss by ignition)..... , ...	7·71	Assiniboine water.
2. Calcic sulphate.......................................	4·39	
3. Calcic carbonate	7·05	
4. Iron, alumina and silica..., ...	1·09	
5. Alkaline salts, chiefly as chlorides.................	9·75	
6. Magnesia sulphate....................................	7·81	
	30·09	
	37·80	

Hardness by Clarke's scale, 10·5°.

WATER OF THE RED RIVER IN 1873.

	Total solid contents in grains per Imperial gallon.	
1. Organic matter (loss by ignition)................. ·......	5·28	Red River water.
1. Calcic sulphate.....................................	2·42	
3. Calcic carbonate............	10·50	
4. Iron and alumina, 2·80 ; silica, ·98................	3·78	
5. Alkaline salts, chiefly as chlorides................	5·18	
	21.88	
	27·16	

Hardness by Clarke's scale, 9°.

It will be observed from the above analyses that (all things consid- Comparison of waters.
ered) the water of the Red River is rather better than that of the
Assiniboine. This, I think, is contrary to the general belief, owing to
the greater quantity of mechanically suspended impurities in the Red
River water. The amount of organic matter in both is considerable,
and would, no doubt, be greater in fresh samples.

· They contain a large quantity of lime salts, the carbonate pre- Relative composition.
dominating in the Red River, while the Assiniboine has the most
sulphate. Magnesia sulphate does not appear to be present in appre-
ciable quantity in the water of the Red River, while its occurrence in
so large a proportion in the Assiniboine water constitutes its worst
feature. If the Red River in any part of its course contained magnesia
sulphate, its absence in the stream near Fort Garry at the above date
may be accounted for by its having been precipitated by the carbonate
of iron contained in springs and surface water flowing into the river,
or by the carbonate of potash resulting from the lixiviation of the
ashes left by the extensive burning of the timber belt going on almost
every year along the course of the river. And this suggests a means
by which the Assiniboine water might be freed of its Epsom salts, in

case it should be found otherwise desirable for the supply of the city, namely, by adding to it a certain amount of wood ashes, which could easily be obtained so long as wood is so largely used as fuel. In this way a salubrious salt, the sulphate of potash, would be substituted in the water for one which Dr. Parkes, the well-known writer on sanitary science, says should not exceed three grains to the gallon in a wholesome water.

Stage of water when samples were collected. The samples of water analysed by Dr. Edwards were collected after a long term of dry autumn weather, and at a time when both rivers were rather low. They would, therefore, represent the average composition of the streams better than if they had been collected at any other season. During the spring freshet the waters would contain a larger proportion of organic matter relatively to the mineral salts, in summer they would be affected locally and temporally by the wash from thunderstorms, while during the winter they would be exceptionally pure.

I might mention in connection with this subject that the same year in which I brought home the above samples of water, I collected specimens of the white efflorescing salt or "alkali" which every traveller observes around many of the lakes and covering the dry beds of ponds in the region drained by the western branch of the Assiniboine, and found that it consists principally of sulphate of sodium and magnesium, together with chlorides of calcium and sodium.

"Alkali" of the region drained by the Assiniboine.

Improvement of the water. As to the possibility of improving either of these waters before distributing them in the city, I may remark that, while much of the coarser matter held in suspension might be thrown down in settling ponds, a portion of it is so very fine that it cannot be got rid of in this way. The turbid water of the Red River imparts a muddy appearance to the whole length of Lake Winnipeg, notwithstanding the immense volume of clearer water supplied by the Winnipeg River, and along with the milky Saskatchewan it is discharged by the Nelson River into the sea—still very muddy—700 miles from the city of Winnipeg.

Filtration. Filtration is the only effective remedy for this defect, and in addition to the sand and gravel for removing the mechanical impurities, there should be a layer of animal charcoal for eliminating the organic matters. Such a provision would add comparatively little to the cost of filtration, since this substance is found in practice to act efficiently in such cases for a great length of time. Unfiltered river waters, more than any other kind, are frequently the medium for propagating such diseases as typhoid fever, cholera, diarrhœa, dysentry, internal parasites, &c., by means of the living germs which they contain, and

Propagation of diseases.

which multiply with extraordinary rapidity in the warm weather.
The danger arising from this cause will increase in the case of the
rivers under consideration, as the districts through which they flow
become more thickly inhabited. Almost the entire area drained by Geology of the
the Assiniboine is believed to be underlaid by soft flat-lying rocks of river basins.
Cretaceous age, while the basin of the Red River lies principally on
Silurian strata. Its largest branch, however, the Red Lake River,
which flows from the eastward, rises in the metamorphic region to the
west of Lake Superior.

A supply of better water might be brought down at some future Other possible
sources of
time from one of the clear streams of the Pembina or the Riding supply.
Mountain; or it might be conveyed from the Broken-head, White-
mouth or Winnipeg River, or even from the Lake of the Woods
(which lies at a very considerable elevation above the Lower Red
River Valley,) should the city become sufficiently populous and wealthy
to afford the great expense which would be involved in the operation.
The streams flowing entirely through the Laurentian country, beyond
the Winnipeg, could, no doubt, furnish a still purer and softer water
than any of the sources which have just been mentioned.

A large amount of rain falls in Winnipeg, especially in the months
Rain water.
of May and June, and probably the quantity of most excellent soft
water which is shed from the roof of every house and lost, if husbanded,
would prove sufficient for the wants of its occupants. In order to
preserve this supply, a large cistern might be dug below the bottom Cisterns.
of the cellar floor, so as to protect the water from frost in winter and
evaporation in summer. This should be lined with hydraulic cement
and covered with iron, over which a thick layer of earth ought to be
spread. A quantity of scrap iron might be placed in the bottom.
The only openings should be those admitting the feed-pipe and pump-
tube. The water might be made to pass through a filtering box before
entering the cistern. If the cellar should be liable to be flooded, the
upper part of the cistern might be puddled all round after the manner
adopted by miners to keep out water.

It may be interesting to compare the waters of the Red River and Comparison
with waters
the Assineboine with those of rivers in other parts of the world, both European
in regard to their solid constituents and to their hardness. The fol- rivers.
lowing list shows the number of grains of solid matter, of all kinds,
per gallon, in a number of the rivers of Europe:—Thames, above
London, 15 to 18·5; Seine, at Paris, 20·0; Rhine, at Lyons, 12·88;
Garonne, at Toulouse, 9·56; Loire, at Mehung, 9·52; Scheldt, in Bel-
gium, 20·49; Rhine, at Basle, 11·97; Spree, at Berlin, 8·0; Danube,
at Vienna, 10·15,

St. Lawrence and Ottawa waters. Dr. T. Sterry Hunt found the clear water of the St. Lawrence at the Cascades to contain 11·74 grains of solids to the gallon, while the brown water of the Ottawa at St. Anne's contained only 4·84 grains, the colouring being due to a minute quantity of vegetable matter derived from swamps at the head waters of the river, while the invisible impurities of the St. Lawrence consisted mainly of mineral salts.

Hardness. The hardness of the St. Lawrence at the Cascades was found by Dr. Edwards to be 3·5°, and of the Ottawa at St. Anne's 2·5°, while that of the mixed water of the two rivers supplied to Montreal varied from 2° to 3° according to the season of the year. The Assiniboine and the Red River waters, although harder than those of the St. Lawrence or Ottawa, are not much worse in this respect than much of the water supplied to towns in England, as shown by the following examples taken from Dr. Wanklyn's treatise on *Water Analysis:*—The Thames, above London, 14°; Castleton, Derbyshire (water supply), 11°; Oxton, Birkenhead, 11·9°; Chelmsford, Essex, 13·3°; Kirbyshore, Westmoreland, 22°; Chatham, 24°.

GEOLOGICAL AND GENERAL DESCRIPTION OF THE REGIONS EXPLORED.

Owing to the uniformity in the geological character of large areas of the region which I passed over, and the total absence for long distances of any rocks older than the drift, this report may be shortened and simplified by including a notice of the geological observations in the general account of the season's operations. This will be arranged in the order in which the work was performed, as already indicated.

Continuation of previous survey of Nelson River The track-survey which I made in 1878 of the upper part of the Nelson River, terminated at the Goose-hunting River, about half way from Lake Winnipeg to the sea. On my way to the Churchill River I resumed the survey of the Nelson at this point, and continued it to Split Lake, the direction being nearly north and the distance about nine miles. Grand Rapid occurs at four miles in a straight line before coming to the lake, and has a descent of about fifteen feet in the form of a steep chute. This is apparently the only formidable obstruction to the navigation of the Nelson River from the south-west extremity of Sipi-wesk Lake, or from Red Rocks Rapid, on another channel, all the way to the foot of Gull Lake, a distance of about 160 miles. A portage of less than 200 yards in length, over a steep ridge of clay and rock, leads past this chute, at the foot of which the river makes a short western "jog" and receives the Grand River on the left side. At a mile and a half below the "jog" the Nelson gives off a large channel or discharge to the right, which flows north-east into Split Lake. The

The Grand Rapid.

Navigable stretch.

Lower Chain-of-Rocks (or Islands) Rapid, with a descent of only about two feet, occurs one mile further down.

Between the Grand Rapid and the western part of Split Lake the gneiss is partly reddish and partly grey and hornblendic. The strike varies in different places from S. 60° to S. 80° W. It is cut by a number of dykes of dark-coloured diorite, some of which, just below the junction of the Grass River, are very large. Their run has a general north-and-south tendency. On the north side of Split Lake, opposite the two inlets of the Nelson, the gneiss is cut by numerous dykes of all sizes and running in many directions. Below Chain-of-Rocks Rapid, on the north-west side of the river, dark grey quartzite and hornblendic schist occur, and also a dark green serpentinous-looking rock with a somewhat schistose structure. The Burntwood River, a large stream, with turbid water like that of the Nelson, enters the western extremity of Split Lake. On each side of the mouth of this river, the rocks consist of quartzose, felsitic and hornblendic slates, running west-south-west, much cut up by trap dykes. At the Island of the Dead, in the entrance of the river, hornblendic schist is interstratified with ribboned quartzite, striking east and west. The rocks on some islands about a mile north-east of the western or principal inlet of the Nelson River, consist of dark bluish-green hornblende and mica schist, interstratified with ribboned gneissic bands and with irregular layers of softer, light green schist, all much contorted. The rocks of the point between the Nelson and Burntwood rivers, and the islands for two miles to the north-west of it, may be considered as Huronian, but beyond this, in the same direction, they pass into gneiss, consisting of thin hornblendic and micaceous layers, alternating with others of quartz.

Gneiss.
Dykes.
Schists.
Burntwood River.
Schists.
Huronian.

Split Lake runs east-north-east, and is about twenty-five miles long by two or three wide. The rocks along its northern shore consist of gneiss, which is generally of a hornblendic character, interstratified with quartzose layers. Towards the west end the strike is about east and west, but elsewhere it is much disturbed. Besides the rocks of Huronian character just described as occurring at this extremity of the lake, a green hornblende rock, which was met with on an island near the east end, may be of the same age. What appears to be another limited area of Huronian rocks in this part of the country, is met with on the south side of the Grass River where it joins the Nelson. Here, at about half a mile west of the Grand Rapid portage, there is a ribboned, slaty, hornblendic rock, together with a coarse variety, and a dark gray quartzite, dipping S. 20° W. < 60°. These are cut by a great dioritic dyke, running about north and south. Siliceous and

Split Lake.
Probable Huronian on Grass River.

2

hornblendic slates are found to the west of this, but at about four miles from Grand Rapid portage rusty quartzose gneiss which is believed to be Laurentian, appears, dipping S. 40° E. < 60°.

Country around Split Lake. The country around Split Lake presents a generally even, but slightly undulating outline. The immediate shore-line is usually rock-bound, but on ascending this a deposit of brownish clay, which appears to afford a good soil, is found to be spread over the country. The tops of the larger and higher islands in the lake are also covered with the same deposit.

Temperature of water. On the 24th of July the water of Split Lake had a temperature of 69°, and on the 11th of September of 59° Fah.

Elevation. According to my barometric observations, Split Lake would have an elevation of 440 feet above the sea.

In order to reach the waters of the Churchill River we ascended a creek on the north side of Split Lake, about half way from its west end, and from it made a portage a mile long in a north-westerly direction, over a nearly level surface of brownish clay with small spots of sphagnum, to a pond, from which another portage, one-third of a mile

Split Lake to Assean Lake. long, with the same bearing, brought us to the shore of Assean Lake, which runs at right angles to the portage trail. The north-eastern part of this lake, which we followed from the portage to the outlet, a distance of nearly seven miles, is narrow and straight. The lake is said to run about an equal distance south-westward from the portage, and it must therefore have a total length of about thirteen miles. It has an elevation of about twenty feet above Split Lake. The rock on either side of the portion which we followed is gneiss, with a general north-and-south strike.

Leaving Assean Lake we followed a small, crooked stream called the O-na-ton-wi for a distance of eight miles northward, in a straight line,

Assean Lake to Was-kai-ow-a-ka Lake. to a small lake of the same name. From this we reached the south end of Was-kai-ow-a-ka Lake, at the head of the Little Churchill River, by a chain of seven portages and six lakes running north-westward, the whole distance being about seven miles in a straight line. The country traversed consists of brownish-grey clay, which presents steep banks on some of the lakes, in one case eight feet high. Where the ground is level it is covered with wet sphagnum.

Was-kai-ow-a-ka Lake. The eastern division of Was-kai-ow-a-ka Lake runs nearly north, and has a length of about twelve miles. The outlet is on the east side, about eight miles from the southern extremity, at which it receives a stream; and another, called Pickerel River, enters the north end. Opposite to the outlet, a narrow channel connects this with an extension of the lake, which the Indians informed me runs south-eastward six or seven miles, and has a width of three or four miles. The south-eastern shore

From a Photograph by DR. R. BELL.

VIEW UP THE LITTLE CHURCHILL RIVER, TEN MILES ABOVE RECLUSE LAKE.

SHEWING GENERAL CHARACTER OF COUNTRY.

of the lake washes the base of a ridge of drift, which extends for some
miles to the north-east and south-west, and presents a bare bank of
clay rising about sixty feet above the water, from which the lake
derives its name. The water is clear, and on the 26th of July it had a
temperature of 67° Fah. It abounds with fish, including grey trout, Fish.
some of which are very large, whitefish, pike, pickerel, dog-fish and
suckers. Its elevation above the sea appears from my barometrical Elevation.
observations to be 936 feet. The country around is green, the timber
consisting of spruce, white birch, aspen, balsam-poplar and tamarac. Timber.

The general course of the Little Churchill River, all the way from Little
the southern extremity of Was-kai-ow-a-ka Lake to its junction with Churchill River
the Great Churchill, is nearly north-east, and the distance between the
points about ninety miles in a straight line. For three miles below the
outlet the river has a tranquil course, and then expands into a small
lake, but below this, for some seventeen miles, it is broken, here and
there, by rapids, past some of which short portages require to be Rapids.
made. Solid-gneiss rock occurs at the rapids, but elsewhere the banks
consist of clay, gravel or sand. Further on the river flows for a few
miles with a gentle current, among islands and lagoons, with occasional
banks of clay, covered in some places with peat four feet thick. The
accompanying wood-cut is from a photograph taken at the lower end Wood-cut.
of this stretch, looking up-stream. At thirty-eight miles from the
southern extremity of Was-kai-ow-a-ka Lake, the Switching River
falls in from the left side, and at five miles further we enter the Recluse Recluse Lakes.
Lakes, which are of small size and connected by a short sluggish portion of the river. So far the woods along the river have been generally
green, but below these lakes the timber is mostly burnt all the way to Burnt country.
the Great Churchill.

The rock of the east side of Was-kai-ow-a-ka Lake is a coarsely Syenitic gneiss.
crystalline, massive, greyish-red syenitic gneiss, but along the river,
especially in the first twenty miles below the lake, other varities of
gneiss are exposed at the rapids. The strike is not uniform, but in most
cases it approaches a south-westward direction. The Recluse Lakes lie
in the north-eastern part of a valley four miles wide, excavated in the
great clay deposit which is everywhere spread over this region. Along Clay deposit.
the north-west side the banks are from 100 to 150 feet high. On leaving
the lakes a few rapids occur, but below these, the river, for a long distance, flows in a crooked channel of uniform breadth with a tolerably
swift current, between banks of clay, varying from twenty to one
hundred and fifty feet in height, but averaging from forty to fifty feet.
The upper part of this deposit appears to be a modified clay, with
occasional layers of gravel, and sometimes a ridge of gravel and sand

above it; while the lower part is unstratified and full of pebbles, with some boulders. The latter comprise yellowish-grey magnesian lime-

Boulders. stone of Silurian age, gneiss, and a great variety of rocks belonging to the unaltered, unfossiliferous series of the east coast of Hudson's Bay, which resembles the Nipigon group and which have been described in my report for 1877. Boulders of these rocks are abundant around Was-kai-ow-a-ka Lake and they were also observed along the Nelson River. Limestone gravel became abundant a few miles below Was-kai-ow-a-ka Lake.

In approaching the Great Churchill, the river, for a number of miles, is deep and smooth, and the clay banks have retired to a considerable **River waters.** distance on both sides. The water of this stream has a brownish tinge and forms a striking contrast with that of the great river into which it falls. The latter is bright and clear, like the St. Lawrence water, and on the 3rd of August it had a temperature of 62° Fah. During the few days preceding this date, the temperature of the Little **Churchill River** Churchill averaged 63° Fah. Just below the junction or "forks" the **at junction of** river is nearly a mile wide, and the land on the east side rises from **Little Churchill** 300 to 450 feet above its level. No rock appears in these high banks, which are evidently composed of drift. Immediately above the forks the river is much narrower, and the clay banks on both sides rise steeply to a height of about 150 feet. The latitude of the north-west side of the river, opposite the mouth of the Little Churchill, I found to be 57° 30' 57", and the variation of the compass at this locality to be about 12° 30' E. On the latter stream, at twenty miles south of the junction, the variation was ascertained to be 10° 30' E., and at twenty-four miles it was 11° 30' E.

Churchill River I ascended the Churchill for a distance of twenty-three miles (fol-**above the** lowing the stream) from the mouth of the Little Churchill. In this **"Forks."** distance it averaged about one-third of a mile in width and had high banks of clay on alternate sides. Numerous rapids were met with, and the total rise in the above distance amounted to 173 feet, or at the rate of seven and a-half feet per mile. A perpendicular fall, remarkable for its great width, was reported by an old Indian whom we met at Norway House to occur at no great distance further up the river. The upward course of the river beyond the point which I reached, must be nearly parallel to the Little Churchill, as the Indians say that in the winter the vapor from the falls all along this section can be seen from the latter river and Was-kai-ow-a-ka Lake. The fundamental rocks are exposed in the bed of the river at the rapids, and consist of coarse **Syenitic gneiss.** greyish-red or light reddish syenitic gneiss, like that of Was-kai-ow-a-ka Lake, and in some parts porphyritic, passing into a somewhat fine-

LOW TIDE AT NEW FORT CHURCHILL.
ESKIMO DOGS IN THE FOREGROUND.

grained red gneiss resembling a hard altered red sandstone. Both
rocks have a very "dry" character. The general strike is north-
eastward or across the strike of the river.

The distance from the junction of the Little Churchill to the mouth Lower part of
of the river, according to my survey, is about 105 miles in a straight Churchill River
line, and the bearing about N. 33° E. (ast.) A considerable stream
enters from the left side at twenty miles below the Little Churchill;
but with this exception the tributaries are apparently all small. For
the first twenty-five miles in a straight course below the point just
mentioned, the river bends about a good deal, but from thence it makes
only two (nearly straight) reaches to the sea. From the forks to the
end of the first of these, the average width of the river is about half a
mile, and few islands occur, but in the last reach, islands are numerous,
and the width, for a considerable distance, is upwards of two miles.
The tide extends to the foot of the last rapid, a distance of seven or
eight miles from the open sea, the intervening section forming a lagoon Lagoon.
about two miles broad. The mouth of the river, which is bounded by
solid rock, is less that half a mile in width, and the point on the west
side projects some distance beyond the other. The fine harbour of Churchill
Churchill lies immediately within the mouth of the river. Harbor.

From half a dozen barometric observations, taken on three different
days, I found the river, where it is joined by the Little Churchill, to be
705 feet above the sea. This would give an average descent of rather Descent in
more than seven feet per mile to the head of tide water. Rapids are river.
numerous, especially in the first thirty miles, and again in the neighborhood of the angle formed by the last two stretches of the river at forty
miles from the mouth. Only one of them, however, is formidable Only one
enough to require a portage to be made. This is a steep rapid, which portage.
may be called the Portage Chute, situated at twenty-eight miles, in a
straight line, below the forks. Here the canoes are carried a distance
of 205 paces on the south side of the river.

In the first twenty-five miles above referred to, in which the river is
more crooked than elsewhere, it runs from side to side in a valley two Deep valley.
to four miles in width, of which the slopes, consisting of earth, rise to
heights of two or three hundred feet above the water. Beyond this
distance, the high banks disappear or recede further from the river.

The same coarse reddish syenitic gneiss which was found above the Syenitic gneiss.
forks continued to be met with in the bed of the river at almost every
rapid for a distance of thirty-five miles, in a straight line, downward
from this point. In some places it was porphyritic from the presence
of large crystals of salmon-coloured feldspar. The strike could scarcely
be recognized. At one place it appeared to be W. N. W.

Rusty sandstone.

At the end of the twenty-five miles from the forks, a rather coarse greyish rusty sandstone, in horizontal beds, makes its appearance on the right side of the river, and continues for three miles, or to the Portage Chute above referred to. In one place it forms a cliff twenty feet in height, and rests upon the red syenitic gneiss which is here seen in the bottom of the river.

Cliff of earthy limestone.

On the opposite, or left side of the river, a cliff of greyish-buff very crumbling earthy limestone or calcareous marl begins at the Portage Chute, and continues for eight miles downward with a height varying from thirty to fifty feet. In this interval the same rock crops out in a few places on the opposite side of the river from beneath the drift clay, which is also heaped above the beds forming the cliff on the left side.

Illustration.

The accompanying view, looking down the river, is copied from a photograph taken two miles and a half below the Portage Chute, and

Last gneiss.

shows the appearance of the banks in this vicinity. The last of the red syenitic gneiss is seen in a rapid at the termination of the long

A second limestone cliff.

limestone cliff above described. Here another escarpment of the marly limestone, like the one just passed on the left side, and of about the same height, begins on the right side of the river and continues for upwards of four miles, while the opposite bank consists of drift clay with the limestone exposed in one place. Thin irregular and interrupted beds of tolerably pure grey limestone occur among the marly strata. The only fossils observed were some fragments of encrinal stems and casts of *Leptæna*.

Banks of limestone and drift clay.

The termination of this lowermost cliff is about seventy miles from the mouth of the river. Between it and the commencement of the last stretch, a distance of upwards of thirty miles, the banks are from seventy to one hundred and fifty feet high, and consist of drift clay with the limestone cropping out here and there at the base on either side. The latter is likewise exposed at a short distance back from the main banks in the ravines cut by numerous tributary brooks. The limestone also occasionally extends across the bed of the river. The channel of the Churchill in this section is evidently of pre-glacial origin. Along it a considerable thickness of drift rests upon the uneven surface of the limestone, filling its inequalities with a mixture of boulders, gravel and clay. The undisturbed pebbly and bouldery clay is also sometimes observed to fill the angle between the ancient cliff and the river bed.

Along this part of the stream the limestone becomes less earthy and of a dolomitic character. Some of the stronger beds are mottled with white chalky nodules, while others have straggling dark-colored patches running over their surfaces. At the commencement of the last reach, or forty miles from the mouth of the river, the rock becomes more

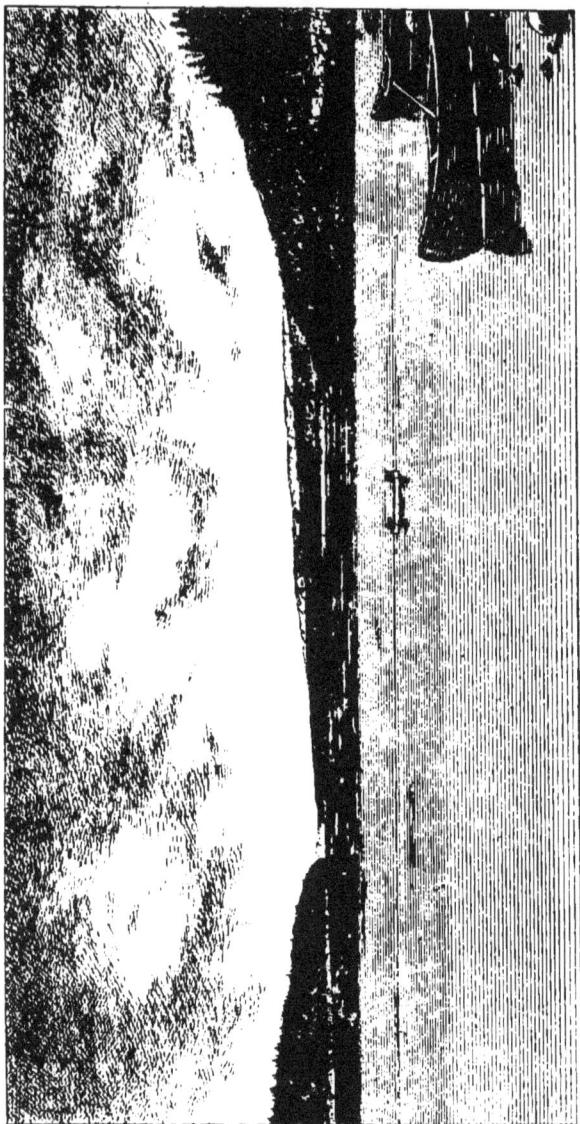

VIEW DOWN THE GREAT CHURCHILL RIVER.
SHEWING LIMESTONE CLIFF AND CLAY BANKS.

From a Photograph by DR. R. BELL.

The Burland Litho'graphic Co. Montreal

evenly bedded and of a lighter grey or buff color. The last observed Buff-colored exposure of the dolomite occurs about five miles further down. No dolomite. fossils were found in this vicinity.

Beginning at thirty miles from the mouth and extending downward for ten miles, the river spreads out among a great number of islands, Islands in the and below this, as far as the tidal lagoon, it is broad, shallow and much river. interrupted with gravelly and bouldery rapids, the last of which is opposite to Mosquito Point, between seven and eight miles from the mouth. The flat-lying limestones or dolomites do not extend to the The limestones sea-coast on the Churchill, as they evidently do on the Hayes and do not reach Nelson Rivers. Westward of the lagoon, and on both sides of the mouth of the river, a different formation makes its appearance. This consists of a massive dark grey quartzite, which seems to contain more Grey quartzite. or less felspar or argillaceous matter, and weathers to a lighter grey on old surfaces. It is easily broken in any direction, and seldom shows distinct traces of bedding. It holds a good many straggling, irregular and short veins of white and grey quartz, with others of a tolerably Quartz veins. regular character. Nearly all these contain scales of specular iron. Specks of iron pyrites were found in some of them, and traces of green carbonate of copper in one. In another of these veins, about two miles east of the mouth of the river, I found small specimens of a blue mineral which appears to be lazulite. Specimens from a number of Lazulite. these veins were brought home to be assayed for the precious metals, and are reported on by Mr. Hoffmann.

On the west side of the river the strike of the quartzite, formation Attitude of appears to be to the south-westward, and on the east side to the south- quartzite formation. eastward, as if the strata were forming the opposite sides of an anti- clinal axis, running down the lagoon and tending to terminate north- ward of the mouth of the river. At Fort Churchill the quartzite is very massive, and the strike is apparently S. 25° W. On the coast, about a mile and a half eastward of the river, it appears to be S. 45° E (mag). At a mile still further east it is quite distinct, and runs S. 75° E. Here the quartzite holds an occasional rounded quartz pebble. On Eagle Nest Point, about seven miles eastward of the mouth of the river, the strike, as shown by a bed containing small rounded pebbles of white quartz, is N. 75° E.

The geological age of these rocks cannot be accurately determined Age of the from present data. They contain no fossils, and are a considerable quartzite formation. distance from the limestones already described as occurring further up the river, and which, no doubt, belong to the Lower Silurian system. They resemble the gold-bearing quartzites or "whin-rocks" of Nova Scotia (which are apparently Lower Cambrian) more closely than any other strata which I have seen. As a convenient name for present purposes they might be called the Churchill quartzites.

Peat.

Peat of fair quality, and perhaps of sufficient thickness to be of economic value, was noticed in several places along the route from Split Lake to Fort Churchill. The following localities may be mentioned:—Creek north of Hudson's Bay Company's post, Split Lake; outlet of Assean Lake; southern part of Was-kai-ow-a-ka Lake, both sides; lagoons twelve miles south of Recluse Lakes, four feet thick on top of bank; Churchill River, twenty-one miles below the forks, five feet thick on top of bank. For some distance above and below the commencement of the last stretch, the woods occur only in patches in an open peaty country as far as can be seen along the river.

Grassy spaces.

Among the islands further down, bouldery and grassy spaces extend between those which are left dry at low water. For a distance of eighteen miles before reaching the mouth of the river, open grassy flats extend for a considerable but irregular breadth on either side.

Illustration.

This open country is said to resemble the barren grounds which begin to the northwestward of Fort Churchill, and are represented in the accompanying illustration taken from a photograph.

Spring ice.

The upper branches of the Churchill being in a warmer region than the lower part of the river, the water rises in spring and bursts away the ice in the latter, while it still retains its strength. This circumstance, and the rapid nature of the river, evidently cause great packing and shoving of the ice during the freshet, and this no doubt has the effect of temporarily damming back the water in many places. Below

Bare sloping banks.

the junction of the Little Churchill the banks are entirely denuded of timber, and have an even and uniform slope up to a height of twenty or thirty, and sometimes even forty feet above the summer-level of the river. The ice would also appear to extend annually to the valleys of the tributary streams, preventing the growth of timber along their sides for a considerable distance back from the main river. During the summer, however, a luxuriant growth of grass and other plants springs up, and covers these sloping banks in most places with a rich green. Further down, after the river has expanded among the islands and the banks have become lower, the effects of the spring ice are no longer noticeable.

Marine shells in the drift.

Marine shells were first noticed in the drift at sixty miles from the mouth of the river. The locality was towards the top of a bank, about 150 feet high, on the right side. The river at the base, from barometrical observation, was 200 feet above the sea, so that these shells probably occur at an elevation of nearly 350 feet above the same level. As the bank, (which consists of pebbly grey clay with apparently a

Elevation above the sea.

VIEW OVER THE BARREN GROUNDS, NORTH-WEST OF CHURCHILL.

With Chippewyan Camp in the Foreground.

From a Photograph by DR. R. BELL.

capping of modified clay,) continued, with the same characters, for a long distance up stream, I have no doubt the shells may be found at a greater distance inland than that at which they were observed by myself. The species noticed at this locality were *Mya arenaria*, M. *truncata*, *Saxicava rugosa*, and *Tellina proxima*. Among the islands further down, where the banks have diminished to about seventy feet in height and the bed of the river has descended to within 100 feet of the sea-level, *Pecten Islandicus* and *Cardium Islandicum* were found in addition to the foregoing species. These shells, together with *Rhynchonella psittacea*, were very abundant in the clay forming the bed of the lagoon at Fort Churchill. Shells in clay at sea-level.

The comparatively rapid elevation of the land, or retiring of the sea, around James Bay and at York Factory was referred to in my reports for 1877 and 1878. The same phenomenon is also noticeable at Fort Churchill. From various circumstances connected with the history of old Fort Prince of Wales, at the mouth of the river, and other data, I conclude that the relative level of the sea and land in this vicinity is changing at the rate of about seven feet in a century. This recession of the sea may be due to a general lowering of its level relatively to the land, and partly to the silting up of portions of Hudson's Bay, interrupting the free flow of the tides. Apparent lowering of the sea.

Spruce and tamarac timber are found growing near the sea coast in favourable situations as far as Seal River, beyond which their north-eastern limit curves inland. The spruce, although not growing as a continuous forest quite as far north as Fort Churchill, is still found of sufficient size in the neighbourhood of this post to be used for building houses, boats, &c. The balsam poplar is rare and of small size at Fort Churchill. White birch, which was found on the main river, eighteen miles above the forks, is said to occur at about sixty or seventy miles west of the mouth of the river. Along the direct overland route from Fort Churchill to York Factory the timber is reported to be generally small, and large prairie-like openings are said to occur, in which the ground is dry and covered with grass or other herbage. Timber of the Churchill.

I saw very good potatoes and turnips growing in the garden at Fort Churchill. Previous to the advent of Mr. and Mrs. Spencer, the cultivation of potatoes had not been attempted, and the possibility of raising them at Churchill, when suggested by Mrs. Spencer, was ridiculed by the oldest inhabitants. However, in spite of predictions of certain failure, ground was prepared, seed planted, and a good crop harvested. The experiment has been repeated successfully for seven consecutive years, so that the question of the practicability of cultivating the potato on the shore of Hudson's Bay in this latitude has been pretty well solved. Potatoes grown at Fort Churchill.

Breeding cattle at Churchill. Hay can be cut in abundance in the neighbourhood of Fort Churchill, and cattle thrive well, yet the same ignorance or obstinacy as that above referred to, formerly prevented any attempt being made to breed stock on the spot, so that every fresh animal required had to be brought from some other post. Now, the small herd which is kept at the place is recruited by raising the animals calved at the fort itself. The open grassy land near the sea is practically of unlimited extent. **Pasture.** Much of it is dry and undulating, affording abundance of pasture for the cattle. The butter made by Mrs. Spencer could hardly be excelled **Butter.** for quality and fineness of flavor in any country.

Although I did not succeed in exploring much of the shore of Hudson's Bay to the north-west of the Churchill, enough was seen to give **Coast N. W. of the Churchill.** one a good idea of the nature of the coast. The east shore of Button's Bay, which begins at the point on the west side of the mouth of the river, runs south-westward for nearly ten miles. Fort Churchill is situated on the west side of the lagoon, about five miles from the mouth of the river. From the fort, the distance westward across the penin- **Button's Bay.** sula to Button's Bay I found to be only a little more than two miles. Around the bottom of this bay, and westward, the shore is extremely low. When the tide is out, wide bouldery flats are laid bare. These descend so gradually to the sea level that it is difficult to effect a land- **Flat bouldery shores.** ing, even from a small boat. Looking over these flats, the sky and the even outline of the boulders seem to meet in the distance, and their appearance suggests "a sea of boulders" as an appropriate name for them. Even within the lagoon of the Churchill, when the tide is out, the bouldery flats on either side form a conspicuous feature. Those on **Illustration.** the west are represented in the accompanying illustration, taken from a photograph, looking southward at Fort Churchill. The boulders, which are of all sizes and generally well rounded, comprise a consider- **Derivation of the boulders.** able variety of rocks, the prevailing ones being those of the unaltered group of the east coast of Hudson's Bay in the neighbourhood of Mani- tounuck and Nastopoka Sounds, which, as already stated, resembles the Nipigon series. Boulders of gneiss and fossiliferous yellowish-grey limestone are also numerous. At some places on the shore, within the first few miles to the eastward of the mouth of the Churchill River, **Cream-colour-ed dolomite.** a very light cream-coloured dolomite, resting on the grey quartzite, is so abundant, in a fragmental condition, that I have little doubt it occurs in place immediately beneath, or at no great distance off.

Latitude of (new) Fort Churchill. While waiting at Fort Churchill for the sailing of the Hudson's Bay Company's ship, in order to proceed to York Factory, I obtained the latitude of the place by five different observation of the meridian alti- tude of the sun, taken by Troughton's repeating circle, as follows :—

From a Photograph by DR. R. BELL.

VIEW UP THE LOWER NAVIGABLE PORTION OF THE NELSON RIVER, SIXTY MILES FROM THE SEA.

SMOOTH WATER WITH HIGH BANKS OF DRIFT CLAY.

(1.)	58°	44'	54''·61
(2.)	58°	44'	22''·80
(3.)	58°	44'	31''·70
(4.)	58°	44'	55''·20
(5.)	58°	44'	50''·90
Mean.....	58°	44'	43''·04

The mouth of the river is about 4' further north. I also ascertained that the variation of the compass at this locality is at present about 11° E., but on the river, at twenty-seven miles southward of the mouth, I found it to be only 6° 30'.   Variation of the compass.

Completion of Track Survey of the Nelson River.

On the 27th of August, I left York Factory, and camped on Point of Marsh, or the extremity of Beacon Point, between Hayes and Nelson rivers, and the next morning started to ascend the latter to Lake Winnipeg. My report for 1878 contains a description of the lower part of the Nelson, which was explored during that season. It will not be necessary, therefore, again to describe this section. In regard to the question of the navigation of this stretch of the river, it was stated that the shallowest place discovered by my soundings was at the head of the tide, abreast of "Gillam's " or the Lower Seal Island. When at this locality again, last August, I carefully sounded the whole width of the river and found the deepest water to be ten feet, as before. The bottom consists of shingle, resting apparently on boulder clay, which here forms both banks of the river and the Seal Islands. "Gillam's " Island and the south bank opposite to it were found, by barometer, to have each a height of eighty feet, while the north bank rises to upwards of 100 feet above the river. The boulders and the pebbles of the drift in this neighbourhood are made up largely of the rocks of the supposed equivalent of the Nipigon series of the east side of Hudson's Bay. Specimens of almost every variety of these strata may be picked up along the banks in this part of the river. Three miles above the Seal Islands I found a large piece of white quartz exactly like that of the veins in the grey quartzite of the mouth of the Churchill. It also contained scales of specular iron precisely similar to those of the Churchill veins. At "The Cache," which is on the north side of the river opposite Deer's Island, or sixteen miles from the Seal Islands, there are numerous large and a few immense angular and partially rounded blocks of this grey quartzite. One of them contains some white quartz pebbles similar to those occasionally observed in the rock in place at Churchill. The accompanying illustration, from a photograph taken on the north-west of the river at sixty-three miles from Point of

Ascent of the Nelson River.
Shallowest part of river.
Soundings.
Seal Islands.
Derivation of boulders.
Boulders of Churchill quartzite.
Banks of the lower Nelson.

Marsh (the extremity of Beacon Point), will serve to show the appearance of the clay banks of the Nelson along its lower section.

First Limestone Rapid. The First or Lowest Limestone Rapid proved to be about seventy-seven miles in a straight line from Point of Marsh, or about ninety by the river. The foot of the rapid is in latitude 56° 36′ 6·1″. Here, and at twenty-two miles higher up the river, the variation of the compass is 11° 30′, while at the place where the above photograph was taken it is 8° 45′. Two more strong rapids over limestone occur at nine and ten miles respectively above the lowest one. The first gneiss is seen in the bed of the river ten miles higher up, and the limestone in the banks disappears at two or three miles further on. The high clay escarpments of the lower part of the river continue to the Limestone Rapids, where they still have an elevation of about 100 feet, but they have diminished somewhat where the limestone disappears; and the bare banks skirting the river terminate near the foot of a chute with a perpendicular pitch of twelve feet, sixteen miles above the Third Limestone Rapid. Beyond this, an occasional bank of clay is seen as far as Gull Lake, but around this body of water and up to Split Lake the country appears to be generally pretty level. A few species of marine shells were observed in the upper parts of the clay banks all the way from the mouth of the river to the twelve-feet chute just mentioned. The only species met with at this upper limit were *Saxicava rugosa* and *Tellina proxima*. The elevation, as indicated by barometer, was upwards of 200 feet above the sea.

First gneiss.

Termination of bare clay banks at Twelve-feet Chute.

Marine shells in clay.

Pre-glacial channel. In my report for 1878 it was stated that the lower part of the Nelson River appears to flow in a pre-glacial channel. Evidences of the existence of such a channel were found in various places along the river all the way to Split Lake. It was also mentioned in the report referred to, that the straight portion of the river between this lake and Sipi-wesk lies in a channel scooped out during the glacial period along the course of a great dyke and afterwards filled with pebbly clay. In the neighbourhood of the Limestone Rapids, and for some miles both above and below them, the hard boulder-clay has been excavated in many places and the hollows filled with loose boulders, shingle, gravel, sand and stratified clay. For a number of miles before coming to the First Limestone Rapid the banks on both sides are about 120 feet high and consist generally of unstratified pebbly clay, but at a point on the north-west side, between two and three miles below the rapid, from twenty-five to fifty feet of sand, gravel and cobble-stones rest upon 100 feet of this clay. Close by, to the north-east of this, the river bank consists of yellow-drab fine sandy clay, and a little further on in the same direction it consists of thirty feet of boulders, cobble-stones and

River channel along a great dyke.

Loose shingle, &c., in hollows in boulder clay.

Composition of river banks.

pebbles at the bottom, overlaid by ninety feet of sand and gravel. On *First Limestone Rapid.*
the same side of the river, at the foot of the rapid itself, 100 feet of the
hard drift clay, which here shows uneven joints with rusty surfaces,
rest upon twenty feet of buff-coloured fossiliferous dolomite in nearly *Section of fossiliferous dolomite.*
horizontal beds. It is shaly at the base, but at the top some of the
beds are two feet thick. These hold flinty and white chalky nodules.
A cliff, twenty feet high, of greyish-buff dolomite, mottled with yellow,
runs along the edge of the rapid on the other side of the river. Among
the fossils observed here was an *Orthoceras* two and a-half feet long and *Second Lime-*
six inches in diameter. On the south-east side, just below the Second *stone Rapid.*
Limestone Rapid, nine miles above the first, a cliff, twelve feet high,
at the edge of the river, is formed of horizontal beds of crumbling buff
and greyish dolomite. At about a mile below this locality these beds
were observed to be slightly undulating. At the Third Limestone *Third Lime-*
Rapid the rock is exposed in horizontal beds at the foot of the clay *stone Rapid.*
bank along the south-east side of the river, and consists of bluish-grey,
drab and buff, somewhat arenaceous dolomite. Near the foot of this *Arenaceous*
rapid a considerable stream, which I took to be the Limestone River, *dolomite.*
enters on the opposite side.

For the next eleven miles the river is very swift, and then a rapid,
two miles wide and full of knobs and little ridges of gneiss, begins, and
continues for five miles, or to the Twelve-feet Chute already mentioned. This might be appropriately termed the Broad Rapid. In *Broad Rapid.*
going from the lowest of these rapids to the other, the banks on
both sides diminish from a height of about one hundred feet at *Diminution in height of banks*
the former to about fifty or sixty at the latter; yet the surface of *over river-bed.*
the ground probably slopes in the same direction as the river, the *Slope of river-*
descent in the latter being apparently greater than would be accounted *bed.*
for by the difference in the altitude of the banks, supposing the tops
of the latter to be horizontal. On the north-west side, the clay bank
is quite continuous and almost bare all the way to within a mile of
the Twelve-feet Chute, a distance of over sixteen miles by the river.
Near the Third Limestone Rapid the bank was observed to be more or
less distinctly stratified throughout its whole height. On the opposite
side, the upper part, and sometimes its whole depth, consists of
gravel and sand.

Along the above interval between the rapids, ledges of the dolomite
crop out from beneath the banks here and there on both sides. The
last exposure is on the south-east side at the bottom of the Broad (five
miles) Rapid. Here it is finely arenaceous, of a mottled light bluish- *Arenaceous*
grey color, and holds some of the same fossils as those found further *dolomite.*
down the river. The fossils collected at the three Limestone Rapids

have been examined by Mr. Whiteaves, and his report upon them is given as an appendix. From this it will be seen that we have here most of the species characteristic of the dolomite which occurs along the Red River in Manitoba, and which Mr. Whiteaves regards as equivalent to the lead-bearing limestone of the Western States or about the horizon of the Utica formation. In passing through Manitoba on the way home, I made a considerable addition to our collection of fossils from the banks of the Red River, in the parish of St. Andrew's, and some from the same parish were presented by Mr. William Murdock, C.E.

From the Twelve-feet Chute to the foot of Gull Lake, the distance, in a straight line. is forty-three miles, and the bearing a little south of west. The River in the interval is of very unequal width. Rapids occur in many places, and numerous portages require to be made. In the last four or five miles before entering Gull Lake the worst rapids in the whole course of the Nelson River are encountered. They may for convenience be called the Gull Rapids. The lower chute of this interval has a descent of about fifty feet in less than half a mile, and requires a portage of 900 paces to be made in order to get past it. The upper portion of the Gull Rapids is divided among islands, but its total fall must amount to more than that of the lower chute. Six principal rapids occur between the Twelve-feet Chute and those just described, and the whole ascent in the river in this space cannot be far from 100 feet. About mid-way down this section, the river divides among islands, the largest of which may be about four miles long. Just above these islands, the upward course of the river makes a bend to the southward of about six miles, and then resumes its former course. Nine miles above the Twelve-feet Chute, a brown-water river falls in from the south, which appears to be the largest tributary from that side below Split Lake.

Gull Lake is merely an expansion of the river, and runs with its general course, which has the same bearing (a little south of west) all the way from the commencement of the Laurentian gneiss to the head of Split Lake. It is twelve miles long and four wide in the middle, and contains a few islands. The distance from the head of Gull Lake to the outlet of Split Lake is eighteen miles, and the average width of the river is nearly one mile. An easy rapid, two miles in length, occurs at the outlet of Split Lake, and two short ones about mid-way between the two lakes. An occasional bank of clay is seen along the section of the river under description, but, as already stated, the country in the neighbourhood has a generally level appearance, the only excep-

Fossils examined by Mr. Whiteaves.

Nelson River and Manitoba dolomites of Utica age.

River for 43 miles below Gull Lake.

Gull Rapids.

Six rapids above Twelve-feet Chute.

Islands.

Bend in the river.

Gull Lake.

Slight rapids.

tion being Fox Hill (a part of the ridge running past the south end of Fox Hill.
Was-kai-ow-a-ku Lake), which is visible to the north-westward from
the lower part of Split Lake. The Assean River enters the north side Assean River.
near the outlet, and at a narrow place, just west of it, there is a perceptible current in the lake.

From the termination of the fossiliferous dolomites to the outlet of
Split Lake, the rocks along the Nelson River consist of Laurentian Laurentian.
gneiss and schists, with the exception of a small area of what appear
to be Huronian strata at the foot of the lowest Gull Rapid. At a Huronian at
point on the north side, about one mile below this rapid, a coarse grey Gull Rapids.
mica-schist, with strings and bunches of white quartz along the bedding, dips N. 15° E. < 80°. Crossing the foot of the rapid itself is a
band of fine-grained massive mica-schist, passing into dark grey
quartzite, ribboned with streaks of white quartz and red felspar. The
dip is N. 10° E. < 80°. A dark finely-crystallized diorite, probably
forming part of a dyke, was observed at the sides of the rapid.

The Laurentian gneiss, in the section which has been indicated, Laurentian
presents some variety in composition, color, texture, and in the char- gneiss.
acter of its stratification, which it is unnecessary to describe minutely in
the present report. Sometimes the gneiss passes into hornblende or
mica schist. In a few places the latter is studded with garnets, and it Garnets.
generally contains veins of coarse, light-colored granite. The strike, Granite veins.
Strike.
which was recorded in many places, was nowhere found to preserve a
general uniformity of direction for any considerable distance, but in
the majority of all the cases noted it had a northwesterly tendency.

On the first island above the narrows near the outlet of Split Lake, a Split Lake.
green hornblende rock, which may be Huronian, runs S. 15° W., vertical, and on the east side of the point forming the narrows there is a
peculiar light reddish-grey gneiss, containing a soft chloritic mineral.
The weathered surfaces are very thickly pitted, and have a rough,
spongy appearance. Split Lake and the geology of its shores have
been already referred to in describing my route from Lake Winnipeg
to the mouth of the Churchill River.

Grass River.

Having already surveyed the section of the Nelson River between
the "jog" at the foot of the Grand Rapid and Sipi-wesk Lake, I fol-
lowed the Grass River between these points, in returning to Norway
House, after completing the exploration of the river below Split Lake.
The upward course of the Grass River from its junction with the Upward course
Nelson bears southwestward, nine miles to the outlet of Witchai of river.
("Stinking") Lake, from which it runs southward, or parallel to the

Nelson, for twenty miles, to the Standing-rock Rapid. A canoe-route, seven or eight miles in length, leads from the head of this rapid across to the Nelson. From this rapid the "river" is rather a chain of straggling lakes connected by narrows, with more or less current, for thirty-eight miles in a southwestward direction, to the head of Wintering Lake, where the Pickerel River flows in with the same upward course. About half-way up this stretch, at Burnt Lake, the main branch of the Grass River joins the one we have been following. The short route from Sipi-wesk Lake to Burnt-wood River crosses Wintering Lake at right angles. On the present occasion we followed the part of this route lying between the latter and the outlet of Sipi-wesk Lake. The distance is about fourteen miles in a general eastward direction. From the eastern bay of Wintering Lake we made a portage of one mile and ten chains to the western part of Landing Lake, which discharges into the Nelson River, seven or eight miles below Sipi-wesk Lake. A creek only a few chains in length, entering the south side of Landing Lake, conducted us to a small sheet of water, from which a trail, called Cross Portage, one mile and a third long, brought us to the outlet of Sipi-wesk Lake.

I have already referred to the supposed Huronian rocks at the mouth of the Grass River. At about three miles from the Nelson, a rusty, quartzose variety of gneiss dips S. 40° E. < 60°. For two miles further up, hornblendic gneiss is seen in places, and at the end of this distance it dips S. 10° E. < 80°. Here some large dioritic dykes run across the river. At the first rapid, about seven miles from the mouth, a ribboned felsitic red gneiss has also the same dip.

At the Standing-rock Rapid, a great dioritic dyke crosses the river. It is divided by vertical fissures, one of which has detached from the main rock the mass (shown in the accompanying illustration) to which the rapid owes its name. For about a mile above the rapid, the gneiss, which dips N. 45° W. < 80°, is full of trap dykes. Thence all the way along the route to the outlet of Sipi-wesk Lake, the rocks consist of different varieties of gneiss, often cut by trap dykes. ' The general strike in this interval is southwestward, the directions ranging from about W. to S. 20° W.

The country traversed by the Grass River route between its mouth and Sipi-wesk Lake presents generally an undulating appearance. The land is usually of a clayey nature and the soil often good. There seems to be very little swamp, as far as could be judged by following the canoe-route. Along the river, and around the lakes on its course, the rocks are seen beneath the clay on the islands and ends of points. Half-way up the north-west side of Wintering Lake (which is fourteen

(margin notes)
Chain of straggling lakes.

Wintering Lake.

Wintering Lake to Sipi-wesk.

Landing Lake.

Cross Portage.

Gneiss.

Great dyke at Standing-rock Rapid.

South-westward strike.

Character of country along Grass River.

STANDING-ROCK RAPID, GRASS RIVER, NELSON VALLEY. From a Photograph by DR. R. BELL.

COLUMNAR TRAP OF A LARGE DYKE.

or fifteen miles long) a rocky hill overlooks the water for a few miles. Here, and in some other places on the route, the woods are burnt, but most of the timber in this region appears to be green, and of a thrifty growth, the spruces sometimes measuring over six feet in girth. The water of Grass River is slightly turbid, but that of Landing Lake is clear. The barometer, indicated that this lake has an elevation of thirty-six feet over Wintering Lake, and fifty-four feet over Sipi-wesk Lake.

Elevation of Landing Lake.

EXPLORATIONS BY MR. A. S. COCHRANE.

Finding that the method which would be most advantageous for me to adopt in making my surveys of the Churchill and Nelson Rivers, would not require the aid of my assistant, I assigned to Mr. Cochrane a separate region to explore, in order that by working independently of each other, we might examine a larger area of country during the season. He was instructed to make a topographical and geological exploration of the region lying to the south of the route which I had followed the previous year, using God's and Island Lakes and their connecting waters from Oxford House as a basis of operations. He was also directed to make observations and collect information as to the fauna of the region, the climate, soil, timber, and the character of the country generally.

Instructions.

Region southward of Oxford House.

The accompanying map, on a scale of one inch to four miles, engraved from the original, as prepared by Mr. Cochrane from his own track-surveys, exhibits the leading topographical features of the region which he explored. It serves to simplify very much the following description, which is taken from this gentleman's account, aided by his plans, notes and specimens. He proceeded from Norway House to Oxford House by the Hudson's Bay Company's boats, and at the latter place obtained a canoe and men through the courtesy of Mr. Cuthbert Sinclair, the officer in charge. The route which he followed to God's Lake, leaves a bay on the south side of Knee Lake about sixteen miles from its western extremity, and proceeds by way of Wolf and Wolverine Rivers and Swampy Portage, which is nearly two miles long and terminates on the shore of God's Lake.

Map.

Route to God's Lake.

God's Lake runs north-east and south-west, and has a length of forty-eight miles. Its widest portion measures fourteen miles across. At rather more than half-way up from its north-east extremity, is the Manitouwapa, or Wonderful Narrows, where the lake contracts to a few chains in width, and a current flowing to the north-eastward is perceptible. A canoe-route to Oxford Lake leaves the north-west side of the upper portion of the Lake by way of Touchwood River,

God's Lake.

3

Inlet. which flows into the latter. The river from Island Lake enters the south-western extremity of God's Lake, and here the Long Rapid or Kinoutchewan is encountered. God's Lake does not discharge into **Outlet.** Knee Lake, as hitherto represented on sketch-maps, but by God's River, a large and rapid stream, which, on uniting with the Little Severn from the south, forms the Shamattawa River. The outlet of the lake is on the north side, about mid-way between Swampy Portage and its north-east extremity. Vermilion Lake lies not far to the **Vermilion Lake.** north-east of the foot of God's Lake and sends its water into God's River, some distance below the lake of the same name. Knife River, **Knife River.** about the same size as Touchwood River, enters the south-east side of the lake twenty miles from its north-east extremity.

God's Lake, being comparatively free from islands, presents to the eye a greater expanse of water than any other in this part of the country, but Island Lake is about one third larger. The region **Surrounding country.** around God's Lake, as far as can be judged from its appearance from the lake, is rocky but mainly level, and the surface of the water lies, apparently, only about fifty feet, or less, below the general surface of the land immediately surrounding the lake. Between Knife River and Manitouwapa, a distance of eight miles, the bank is higher than **High shore.** usual, the rocks in some places rising as much as 200 feet above the level of the lake. The timber has been burnt at different times over **Burnt timber.** more than half of the tract visible from the lake, and the same conditions are said to extend far into the interior all around. The water, **Clear water.** which is clear, is said to be deep throughout most of the lake, and it abounds in fine fish, the more valuable of which are the whitefish and grey trout. Specimens of the latter are occasionally caught of great **Large trout.** size. This circumstance has given origin to the fables told by the Indians of the mythical trout of huge proportions represented as **Origin of the name of the lake.** inhabiting these waters. The present name of the lake has in some way grown out of the legends connected with this supernatural fish.

Having completed his exploration of God's Lake, Mr. Cochrane returned to Oxford House for a new outfit, and then proceeded to Island Lake by way of the route which leaves the eastern extremity **Route from Oxford to Island Lake.** of Oxford Lake and passes through the south-western division of God's Lake. Between these two sheets of water the route traverses Rat, Clearwater, and Touchwood Lake. In order to go from Rat Lake to Clearwater Lake, three portages required to be made (the intervening space being broken by two ponds), namely, the Long Portage, 3759 **Portages.** yards; Ant Portage, 873 yards; and High-hill Portage, 1538 yards. The country between Oxford Lake and the south-western part of God's Lake along this route is not quite so rocky, nor is the timber so much burnt as it is around the latter lake.

The Kinoutchewan or Long Rapids, at the head of God's Lake, are passed by three portages, with a total length of 2460 yards, and a demicharge 1234 yards long. Above these the upward course of Island Lake River turns east-south-east, and passes through the lower part of Beaver-hill Beaver-hill Lake, which stretches to the south-westward about thirty Lake. miles. At the end of this reach of the river there is a short demicharge into a small round lake, from which a portage of 650 yards leads us into another small sheet of water called Goose Lake. The Kinoutchewanoose, or Little Long Rapids, fall into the southern part of this lake, and are surmounted by four portages, having an aggregate length of 957 yards.

From Goose Lake the Island Lake River has a nearly direct upward Island Lake course, bearing southward, all the way to the lake from which it takes River. its name, the distance being twenty-three miles. Its volume is about the same as that of Trout River (between Oxford and Knee Lakes), and its width, which varies much, may average about 200 yards. In some parts of its course it passes between walls and banks of bare gneiss rock, which sometimes rise to the height of fifty feet or rather more. Indeed this character prevails all the way from God's Lake. The rocky parts are the narrowest, and in the intervals between them the river often opens out into reedy and marshy bays with clayey soil around them. The Island Lake post of the Hudson's Bay Company, Post of the in charge of Mr. Linklater (to whom Mr. Cochrane was indebted for H. B. Company. much kindness), stands on an island near the outlet of the lake.

Island Lake lies nearly east and west, and its greatest length is Island Lake. about seventy miles. The main body of the lake, however, measures only forty-eight miles, and has an average width of twelve miles. Both the northern and southern shores curve gently to the south, parallel to one another. The whole form of the main lake, and the positions of the inlet and outlet, present a striking resemblance to the outline of the human stomach and the situations of its orifices. This lake is very appropriately named, being literally filled with islands in Many islands. every part. The aggregate area of these islands is apparently as great as that of the water-surface. The number probably amounts to several thousands, and they present a great variety in form and size, the largest being several miles in length. Mr. Cochrane counted upwards of one thousand adjacent to the main land all around, most of which are indicated on the accompanying map, and the whole of the interior of the lake is studded with an equal profusion.

A narrow and straight bay runs west from near the outlet for a Narrow Bay. distance of nine miles, which, for convenience of description, might be called Narrow Bay. From its northern shore a canoe-route starts to

Old Wife's Lake, and a similar route to Deer's Lake leaves the west side of Island Lake River about two miles above Pelican Rapid. Several deep bays occur on the south side of Island Lake, and one extends from the eastern extremity, a distance estimated to be about eighteen miles, where it receives the Sagawitchewan River, which is believed to be the principal inlet of the lake. The water of this stream and of all the other feeders of the lake is of a dark color, contrasting strongly with the clear water of the lake itself.

The land about Island Lake is level, and has an average elevation above the water of apparently less than fifty feet. The woods in the neighborhood of the lake are mostly green (or unburnt), so that the country presents a more pleasing appearance than that around God's Lake. The proportion of soil to rock is also much greater than in the neighbourhood of the latter lake.

Soil of the District. Large areas of low sandy land occur on Oxford and Knee Lakes, especially on their northern sides. These tracts support a uniform growth of small spruce timber through which the forest fires have generally run. The higher grounds, where not rocky, present usually a stiff light-colored clay, and soil of this description with more or less loam, is found along the valley of the Trout River. Oxford House is situated on a stiff clayey soil, which here produces barley and all kinds of garden vegetables in perfection. This locality is remarkable for its abundance of wild gooseberries, acres of ground in some places being covered with gooseberry bushes. The land to the north of the lake, opposite to Oxford House, rises to an elevation of about 200 feet, and appears to be higher than any other ground in this part of the country. I was informed that it consists entirely of soil underlaid by drift materials, no rock cropping up in the vicinity. Mr. Cochrane estimates that on an average about half the length of the immediate bank or shore-line of God's Lake may consist of rock, while the other half is made up of clay, sand, gravel, swamp and marsh. From the generally level appearance of the country at a distance, and its resemblance to regions which are covered with soil, he thinks it probable that the greater part of the area is overspread with soil or loose material of some kind. Along the route from Jackson Bay, at the east end of Oxford Lake, to the upper part of God's Lake, the country is more diversified than in the neighbourhood of the latter lake. Although the general outline is more uneven, the proportion of rock to other kinds of surface was estimated by Mr. Cochrane to amount to only about one fourth of the whole. The soil or loose materials consist of loam, clay, sand and gravel, or of mixtures of these. Peat and sphagnum are found in the low grounds in many

Margin notes:
Inlet.
Clear water.
Surrounding country.
Soil.
Productiveness
God's Lake.
Route from Jackson Bay.
Peat.

places. On the north-west side of Swampy Lake, below Knee Lake, there is a bed of good peat of considerable extent, which shows a perpendicular face of four or five feet above the level of the water. Peat of fine quality occurs at Clearwater Lake and Swampy Portage Lake. As already mentioned, rocky banks prevail along the Island Lake River, although, at the wider parts, clay and other soils are met with.

Around Island Lake, although the action of the water has, in the Island Lake course of time, washed away the loose materials and earth, leaving the underlying rocks exposed along a great part of the immediate banks, yet on going back a short distance, a covering of good soil is generally met with. After Mr. Cochrane had completed the circuit of Island Lake, and when he was at the Hudson's Bay Company's post near the outlet, I find that he has made the following note in his field-book, under date of 31st August: "The soil I have seen in passing round the Extract from field-book. lake is very good indeed, being generally clay of a light brownish color, mixed, in most places, with a little fine gravel. In nearly every case where I went inland for any distance, the rock seen along the lake shore disappeared or was covered with soil, and the trees were of a larger and better growth than near the water. There is a very good garden at this post, and certainly I have never seen potatoes look better than they do here." The other varieties of soil which Mr. Varieties of soil. Cochrane noticed around this lake include clay, sand, vegetable loam, and sandy and gravelly loam.

Timber of the District. Spruce is the most abundant wood every- Timber. where in this region. Next in order comes aspen, white birch, tamarac, balsam-poplar and Banksian pine. In many places the spruce attains a very good size, and is used in the form of logs and beams for building purposes. It is also sawn into planks and boards for all sorts of carpenter work. The tamarac and Banksian pine sometimes have a diameter of about twenty inches. Balsam-fir is common and of good size around Island Lake, some of the trees measuring nearly four feet in circumference, but it is scarce at God's Lake, and only rarely seen and of small size as far north as Knee Lake. In going southward the rowan or mountain ash was first seen on Island Lake. Ground maple was met with only on the south side of this lake. I may here mention that on the eastern side of Lake Winnipeg, George's Island, off Poplar Island, is the most northern locality at which I have seen this species.

GEOLOGICAL FEATURES OF THE REGION EXPLORED BY MR. COCHRANE.

Laurentian gneiss is the prevailing rock throughout the whole district Geology of the between Knee and Island Lakes. It presents little variety, and no in- district.

Gneiss.

dications of useful minerals were found in this formation. The colour is usually some shade of grey, generally rather light, but sometimes it is reddish-grey, and more rarely a distinct red or pink. The stratification, which in most parts is moderately distinct, is often bent or contorted. In some places the gneiss has a spotted appearance, and occasionally strongly contrasting beds are seen, but, as a rule, it is of a very uniform character. Its average texture is of the medium variety, or rather tending to be fine-grained, but coarse forms are occasionally seen. Judging from the specimens and Mr. Cochrane's description, an

Granite.

area of very light grey, fine-grained granite occurs on the south-east side of God's Lake, about midway between the Narrows and the northeast extremity; and another, probably of small extent, of light grey, coarse granite at the outlet of Beaver-hill Lake. The latter consists of plates of yellow mica in white quartz and feldspar. Both of these localities are surrounded by Laurentian gneiss.

Character and strike of gneiss.

In order to save a more tedious description, the general character and the strike of the gneiss throughout the region explored by Mr. Cochrane is here given in tabular form. It will be evident from this that no prevailing or general direction can be detected in this part of the country. The bearings are all magnetic.

TABLE SHOWING THE GENERAL CHARACTER AND THE STRIKE OF THE GNEISS IN THE REGION TO THE SOUTHWARD OF OXFORD AND KNEE LAKES.

Between Oxford Lake and God's Lake.

1. Five miles up Rat River—Greyish Red ....West.
2. Northern part of Rat Lake—Grey ....West.
3. Three miles N. of southern extremity of Rat Lake—Micaceous, grey, finely ribboned ....West.
4. One mile E. of High-hill Portage, Clear-water Lake—Coarse grey ....S. 22° W.
5. Clear-water Lake, two miles E. of last—Grey..............S. 5° W.
6. Narrows, at centre of Clear-water Lake—Coarse grey........S. 12° W.
7. One mile and a-half S.E. of Narrows, Clear-water Lake—Light reddish and very light grey.............................S. 50° E.
8. Point N. side, centre of Touchwood Lake—Coarse, grey......S. 60° E.

Around God's Lake.

9. On Island, eight miles N. of Kinoutchewan Rapids, W. side— Dark grey ....S. 70° E.
10. On Island, three miles S. of Narrows—Micaceous grey, finely ribboned ....S. 43° E.
11. Island, W. side, three miles N. of Narrows—Grey ....S. 60° W.
12. Island, W. side, four miles N. of Narrows—Grey ....S. 40° E.
13. Point, W. side, seven miles N. of Narrows—Reddish grey :...S. 70° E.
14. Point, entrance to Bay, N.W. corner........................East.

1**5**. Point, S. end of Fishing Eagle River—Finely grained, flesh
coloured..S. 60° E.
16. Eleven miles E. of Swampy Portage ....S. 20° W.
17. Three miles E. of God's River ....S. 52° W.
18. Island, four miles E. of God's River......................East.
19. Point, eight miles E. of God's River—Finely grained ("pepper
and salt")...S. 30° W.
20. Island, nine miles E. of God's River—Finely grained ("pepper
and salt") ....S. 16° E.
21. Point, eighteen miles E. of Narrows.......................East.
22. Island, thirteen miles E. of Narrows—Grey ....S. 45° W.
23. Point, eight miles N.E. of Narrows—Grey..................S. 60° E.
24. Island, six miles E. of Narrows............................S. 63° E.

Along Island Lake River.

25. Head of Kinoutchewan Rapids—Ferruginous, dark coloured,
siliceous, finely crystalline, hornblendic, schistose........S. 80° E.
26. Point on S. shore of Beaver-hill Lake, near outlet—Coarse reddish grey...S. 68° E.
27. Outlet of Beaver-hill Lake—Fine grained, dark grey, micaceous.S. 65° E.
28. Portage at outlet of Goose Lake—Coarse reddish grey ....S. 48° E.
29. Pelican Rapid—Coarse, grey...............................S. 70° W.

Around Island Lake.

30. One mile N. of Hudson Bay Co.'s post—Grey and greyish-red.S. 45° W.
31. Near mouth of Main-land River, head of Narrow Bay—Very
coarse grey ....S. 15° E.
32. Western extremity of main body of lake, just south of Narrow
Bay —Grey ....S. 25° E.
33. Near head of Pipestone Bay...............................S. 70° E.
34. Point between Pipestone and Highway Bays—Fine greenish
grey..East.
35. West shore of Highway Bay, three miles from extremity—
Greenish grey..S. 40° W.
36. Point four miles E. of Highway Bay—Grey ....S. 16° E.
37. South shore, four miles eastward of last—Light grey........East.
38. Island, five miles further east—Light grey ....S. 40° E.
39. Point fourteen miles west of Fox Island—Dark grey ....S. 80° E.
40. Island in Land-locked Bay, twelve miles W. of Fox Island—
Grey ....S. 80° W.
41. Island, six miles west of Fox Island—Dark grey............S. 20° E.
42. Island, five miles west of Fox Island......................S. 18° W.
43. Island, just west of Fox Island—Very coarse, grey..........East.
44. Island, four miles north-east of Fox Island..................S. 65° W.
45. Island, near N. shore, eight miles north of Fox Island.......S. 45° W.
46. Point on N. shore, eighteen miles north-westward of Fox
Island—Grey, and with reddish and greenish spots ....S. 75° E.
47. Point about the middle of the north shore, or twenty miles
from Fox Island—Fine-grained, greenish...............East.

Huronian. Huronian. The large trough of Huronian schists, &c., in which Oxford and Knee Lakes are included, was described in my report for 1878. The strata of the eastern part of the former lake consist of *Schist-conglomerate.* greyish micaceous and more or less calcareous schist-conglomerate, its pebbles, which are well rounded, consisting mostly of granite and opaque white quartz. On Rat River, a short distance south of the old Wesleyan Mission of Jackson Bay, the strike of this rock, which is of the same variety as that of Oxford House, is east and west, and the dip southward at an angle of 86°. The same conglomerate is found also at the head of Trout River, but farther down the stream, is mostly *Grey mica-schist.* grey mica-schist without pebbles. I found beds of magnetic iron ore *Magnetic iron.* interstratified in siliceous slates where Trout River falls into the head of Knee Lake, and not 'far from this locality Mr. Cochrane observed the calcareo-micaceous schist-conglomerate, holding granite pebbles, *Garnets.* associated with finely crystalline black hornblende schist, full of dull garnets as large as peas. No new facts were noted in regard to the Huronian rocks of the shores of Knee Lake.

Huronian on God's Lake. Mr. Cochrane's specimens and notes show that on the shores of the larger division of God's Lake, rocks which we may consider Huronian, occur a short distance west of the outlet, at the eastern extremity and on both sides of the Narrows. About a mile west of the outlet there is a compact, dark, greenish-grey diorite with small quartzite pebbles, running S. 80° W. (mag.) and dipping northward, and on an island about three miles further west dark greyish-green dioritic schist occurs, dipping S. 40° W. Compact dark greenish-grey diorite with a little calcspar in the joints, occurs around the bay at the eastern extremity of the lake. The strike is in various directions, and the dip at different angles from 45° upwards. At the extremity of the first long point on the south-east side of the lake, or about eight miles from the bottom of the bay just referred to, the rocks run nearly east and west, and consist of dark grey felsitic schist, thickly spotted with whitish felspar, giving it a porphyritic appearance, together with a nearly black finely crystalline hornblende schist. On the same side of the lake, three miles north-east of the Narrows, dark green crystalline diorite occurs, with calcspar in the joints. It holds iron pyrites and small veins of quartz. Two miles nearer the Narrows the rock on an island is a massive grey mica schist with glassy spots. The dip is here southward at an angle of 50°. In the Narrows it consists of grey felsitic schist, showing very fine lines of stratification and dipping N. 30° E. < 85°.

Schist on Touchwood Lake. A dark greenish-grey felsitic hornblende-schist occurs on the eastern part of Touchwood Lake, and a similar rock was found on a small island in Clear-water Lake. About the middle of the south-east shore of the upper division of God's Lake, green mica and hornblende schist was met with, dipping W. N. W. < 50°.

The Huronian strata are largely developed around the western part of Island Lake, and they occur again at its eastern extremity. On the shores of the narrow bay, which runs west from the vicinity of the outlet, the following rocks were found : dark grey felsitic schist with fine lines of stratification; dark grey glossy calcareous schist; grey finely ribboned siliceous slate, felsitic and highly calcareous; grey felsitic silicious slate, and a felsitic slate of an olive-grey color. The strike varies from S. 70° to S. 80° W., and the 'dip is northward at various angles from 45° upwards. *Huronian strata around Island Lake.*

On the south side, in the entrance of Pipestone Bay, a long narrow arm, opening off the lake at eighteen miles from the outlet, beds of a grey calcareous, slightly crystalline steatitic schist are associated with dark greenish-grey felsitic and hornblende slates. Here the strike is about S. S. W. Tobacco pipes are carved by the Indians out of the steatitic rock. *Steatitic schist.*

Along the south side of the next bay, or at a distance of twenty-four miles south of the outlet, the principal rock is a green epidotic horn-blende schist. Associated with this are dark green finely crystalline hornblendic and dioritic schists. The dip here is N. 20° W. at a considerable angle. *Green schists.*

Laurentian gneiss occupies the shore between the different localities of Huronian rock which have just been described. The same rock is also found about the outlet of the lake, but at a point on the northern side, four miles south of the outlet, the Huronian system is represented by the siliceous schist-conglomerate which is so largely developed at the east end of Oxford Lake. A grey quartz-rock is found on the next prominent point, four miles south-east of the last. Further up the shore, or sixteen miles from the outlet, a very dark grey diorite was met with, and at about twenty miles the rocks consist of soft grey schist with harder varieties of the same color full of grains of clear vitreous quartz, together with many of iron pyrites. The dip in this neighbourhood is northward at high angles. Fine grained greenish gneiss, having the same dip, was met with two or three miles further east. This may be either Huronian or Laurentian. To the eastward of it, the ordinary grey Laurentian gneiss was found all along the shore as far as the bay at the head of the lake. *Laurentian gneiss.* *Schist-con-glomerate.* *Grey gneiss.*

On Iron Island, which lies close to the north shore between the two localities of Huronian rocks last described, Mr. Cochrane found dark green serpentine, with calcareous joints, along with a hard fine-grained, semi-crystalline rock of a deep green color, as if due to the presence of *Serpentine.*

chromic oxide. As far as I am aware, this is the first locality at which
serpentine has been discovered in the Huronian rocks to the north-
west of Lake Superior. Its association with the great diorite dyke
cutting the gneiss along the Nelson River above Split Lake was
described in my report for 1878. It was also referred to by Dr. Har-
rington in connection with his investigations of the mineralogical
relations of these two rocks. A tobacco-pipe, carved out of a fine
Serpentine from Rein-deer Lake. variety of serpentine, was presented to me by an Indian on the Nelson
River, who said that the stone came from the great Rein-deer Lake, to
the north of the Churchill River, into which it discharges in about
longitude 103°. At the eastern extremity of the main body of Island
Huronian rocks at east end of Island. Lake, the Huronian rocks are again met with in the form of light
bluish-grey calcareous felsitic schist towards the north side, and of
grey quartz-rock towards the south. A quartz vein in this vicinity
contained patches of yellow pearl-spar, but no indications of metallic
ore was found either here or in any other vein around Island Lake.

Relations of Laurentian and Huronian strata. The strike of the Laurentian gneiss in the neighborhood of the
Huronian rocks appears in most cases to correspond nearly with that
of the latter in the vicinity of Oxford and Island Lakes, but around
God's Lake both systems seem to be much disturbed, and it is difficult
to ascertain their relations to each other. From the table already
given, showing the strike of the gneiss in a considerable number of
localities throughout this region, it is evident there is no tendency to
a general uniformity of direction over any considerable extent of
country.

Glacial striæ. The directions of the glacial striæ in forty-four localities, at which
Mr. Cochrane noted them, are given, along with a list of those recorded
by myself in the other parts of the district.

GLACIAL STRIÆ.

Having already referred to the superficial deposits and the glacial
phenomena generally, with the exception of the striæ, in the course of
my description of the regions traversed, it only remains for me to give
the directions of these grooves, which, for the sake of brevity, I shall
state in tabular form. They are all referred to the magnetic meridian.
Distances are given in straight lines.

Little Churchill River.

1. Four miles below outlet of Was-kai-ow-a-ka Lake.......... S. 30° W.
2. Thirteen miles below   "   " .... S. 70° W.
3. Eighteen miles below   "   " .... S. 85° W.
4. Outlet of lower Recluse Lake, various directions from S. 5° W.
    to S. 40° W., also...................................... S. 80° W.

5. Eagle Rapid, two miles in a straight line below the last. Two
sets, both distinct, S. 10° W. and....................... S. 80° W.

Great Churchill River.

6. Six miles above the mouth of the Little Churchill......... S. 5° W.
7. Five miles above the last, S. to .... S. 5° W.
8. Four miles below the mouth of the Little Churchill, S. 10° W.
and ....:...... S. 70° W.
9. At Fort Churchill. (Here, in one place, the walls on opposite
sides of a gap are both grooved.) S. 20° W. to.......... S. 30° W.
10. On the east side of the mouth of the Churchill............. S 10° E.
11. On the coast of Hudson's Bay two and a-half miles eastward
of the river..'. S. 15° W.
12. On the coast of Hudson's Bay five miles eastward of the river. S. 20° E.

Nelson River.

13. Third Limestone Rapid, distinct from S. 40° E. to.......... S. 60° E.
14. Broad Five-miles Rapid, just above the termination of the
horizontal dolomite, S. 5° W., also up the sloping gneiss
S. 45° to S. 65° W. On level surfaces or normal course... S. 40° W.
15. Just above the twelve-feet chute at the head of the rapid last
mentioned .... S. 45° W.
16. Mouth of river from south, eight miles above last locality, or
thirty-four miles below the outlet of Gull Lake.......... S. 55° W.
17. Twenty-eight miles below Gull Lake.................... S. 65° W.
18. South side opposite large island, twenty miles below Gull
Lake.. S. 70° W.
19. Bend in the river, sixteen miles below Gull Lake.......... S. 60° W.
20. Foot of lowest Gull Rapid, newer set S. 45° W , older set.... S. 60° W.
21. Middle Gull Rapid.. S. 70° W.
22. Upper Gull Rapid... S. 80° W.
23. Point midway up south side of Gull Lake................. S. 85° W.
24. Five miles above Gull Lake, S. 60° W. and................ West.
25. Seven miles below outlet of Split Lake................... West.
26. Three miles below outlet of Split Lake................... S. 85° W.
27. Near H. B. Co.'s post, about midway up north shore of Split
Lake, the striæ intersect each other at various angles, but
the average direction is............................... S. 85° W.
28. Mouth of Burntwood River, Split Lake.................. S. 70° W.
29. Western inlet of Nelson River, Split Lake............... S. 70° W.
30. Chain-of-rocks Rapid, three miles above Split Lake, one set,
S. 25° E., the other..................................... S. 70 W.

Grass River Route.

31. Grass River, five miles from the mouth.................... S. 75° W.
32. Outlet of Witchai (Stinking) Lake....................... West.
33. East side Witchai Lake................................... S. 72° W.
34. Grass River, five miles south of Witchai Lake............ S. 70° W.

35. From last locality nearly to Standing-rock Rapid, several
　　places .... S. 70° W.
36. Around Burnt Lake at the forks of Grass River........... S. 70° W.

Sipi-wesk Lake.

37. N.W. side of Sipi-wesk Lake, about ten miles from outlet,
　　S. 30° W. and .... S. 45° W.
38. Islands in the lake, about fourteen miles from outlet....... S. 40° W.
39. Different places about midway up the lake, which is about
　　thirty-five miles long, S. 40° W. to..................... S. 50° W.
40. About six miles from the south-west extremity of the lake.
　　Here the under-surface of an overhanging wall of gneiss
　　is striated .... S. 35° W.

The following are the directions of the striæ in the God's Lake and
Island Lake region, as recorded by Mr. Cochrane, the bearings also
referring to the magnetic meridian :—

Around God's Lake.

1. Island two miles south of entrance of river from Touchwood
　　Lake.. S. 15° W.
2. Point on east shore, opposite river from Touchwood Lake.
　　(One set, S. 8° E.)..................................... S. 8° W.
3. Point at Narrows.................................... S. 70° W.
4. Island three miles north of Narrows .... S. 20° W.
5. Island four miles north of Narrows .... S. 12° W.
6. Point seven miles north of Narrows..................... .. S. 35° W.
7. Entrance of bay at north-west extremity of Lake.......... S. 30° W.
8. Outlet of Wolverine River into Fishing Eagle Lake........ S. 34° W.
9. Point six miles west of God's River (outlet)............., ... S. 44° W.
10. Point two miles west of God's River .... S. 35° W.
11. Island four miles east of God's River.................... S. 25° W.
12. Island eight miles east of God's River............... .:.... S. 18° W.
13. Point nine and a-half miles east of God's River............ S. 10° W.
14. Point eleven and a-half miles east of God's River......... S. 5° W.
15. Island near south-eastern shore, eleven miles east of God's
　　River .... S. 70° W.
16. Point fifteen miles north-east of Knife River .... S. 24° W.
17. Island twelve miles north-east of Knife River............. S. 18° W.
18. Point six miles north-east of Knife River................. South.
19. Point of large island two miles north of Knife River....... S. 16° W.
20. Point eight miles north-east of Narrows .... S. 20° W.
21. Island five miles north-east of Narrows.................. S. 25° W.
22. Point four miles north-east of Narrows .... S. 30° W.

Between Jackson Bay, on Oxford Lake, and southern part of God's Lake.

23. Northern end of Rat Lake .... S. 20° W.
24. Large island two miles from south end of Rat Lake........ S. 30° W.

25. Island in north-west end of Clearwater Lake.............. S. 30° W.
26. At Narrows, Clearwater Lake............................. S. 30° W.
27. Point near south-east extremity of Clearwater Lake........ S. 30° W.
28. Point six miles south-west of outlet of Touchwood Lake... S. 18° W.
29. Point two miles west of outlet of Touchwood Lake......... S. 20° W.

Around Island Lake.

30. Kettle Island, half way up long narrow bay at west end..... South.
31. Small island two miles from southern extremity of Pipestone
    Bay... S. 25° W.
32. Point west side of Highway Bay, four miles from southern
    extremity .... South.
33. Point east side of Highway Bay, three miles from southern
    extremity .... South.
34. Point one mile north-east of portage from Highway Bay.... S. 10° W.
35. Point five miles south-east of portage from Highway Bay... S. 5° W.
36. Island fourteen and a-half miles west of Fox Island....... S. 20° W.
37. Island in landlocked bay, twelve miles south-west of Fox
    Island... S. 8° W.
38. Island one mile east of Fox Island...................... S. 16° W.
39. Point three miles north-east of Fox Island............... S. 16° W.
40. Point on north shore fifteen miles north-west of Fox Island. S. 20° W.
41. Point nineteen miles south-east of H. B. Co.'s Post........ S. 26° W.
42. Point sixteen and a-half miles south-east of H. B. Co.'s Post. S. 6° W.
43. Point on small island seven miles south-east of H. B. Co.'s
    Post .... S. 8° W.

Northern Limits of Forest Trees.

It would be impossible, within the limits of a report like the present, to give all the facts collected with reference to the trees and shrubs of the country explored; still, the information secured in regard to this subject may prove useful for reference at any time hereafter. The timber has already been incidentally alluded to in describing the regions explored, but it may be worth while here to note some facts in regard to the range of the trees whose northern boundaries traverse the part of the country under consideration.

White Spruce—(the " Pine " of Rupert's Land).—This is the most northern coniferous tree. On the east side of Hudson's Bay the last of it is seen on the coast a short distance north of Richmond Gulf. On the west side it terminates about Seal River. Thence its limit runs north-westward, and is reported to cross the McKenzie River about 200 miles below Peel's River.

Tamarac—(also called "Juniper" and "Red Spruce").—On the east side of the bay it accompanies the spruce almost to the extreme limit. It is abundant at York Factory. Along the lower part of the Nelson

River it is of fair size, but on the Churchill it becomes small towards the sea. Its northern limit runs north-westward to the McKenzie River, which it is said to cross below Peel's River.

Banksian Pine—("Cypress.")—This tree appears to attain its greatest perfection on the southern branches of the Albany River, where I have seen large groves with tall straight trunks, free from branches, and about two feet in diameter at the butt. The original forests of the lower part of the valley of the Moose River having been destroyed by fire many years ago, a crop of white birch and poplars now replaces the former coniferous timber, so that the proper northern limits of the different species of the latter can scarcely be defined. A young and healthy growth of Banksian pines was seen on the Missinaibi branch of this river a few miles below "Hell's Gate," but none were observed to the northward in this region. It was abundant along Steel River, but ceased to be noticed on the upper part of Hayes' River. In going up the Nelson River, it was first met with about twenty miles below Gull Lake. It was found on the upper part of the Little Churchill River, and is said to be very abundant along the Great Churchill above the point which I reached, and also around Athabasca Lake. Its northern limit is reported to cross the McKenzie below Peel's River.

Balsam Fir—(also called "Single Spruce" and "Silver Pine").—Abundant around the southern part of James' Bay and on good dry soil along the Albany River. Mr. Cochrane reports it as common around Island Lake, but scarcer on God's Lake. It is rare and of small size at Knee Lake. In going down the Nelson River, it is scarce below the Sea River Falls, and the last tree which I observed was at the outlet of Sipi-wesk Lake. On the Grass River some good-sized trees were seen as far north as the Standing-rock Rapid. It is not a common tree along the east side of Lake Winnipeg, is scarce between that lake and Lakes Manitoba and Winnipegosis, and appears to be absent to the westward of these lakes, although to the north-west it reaches the McKenzie River.

White Cedar.—The northern limit of this species touches the southern extremity of James' Bay, and to the north-westward it crosses the Albany River at some distance from the sea. It is, however, abundant in the upper Albany country and in the Lonely Lake and English River regions. Its northern boundary crosses the Winnipeg River a few miles south of Pine Falls. Near the south end of Lake Winnipeg it is met with, of good size, in the bay to the south of Grand Marais Point. In Manitoba, it is found east of Red River in the Big Woods, and even in Kildonan, from which its western limit runs towards the south-east angle of the Province and thence southward in the United

States. Cedar brushwood grows around Cedar Lake on the Great Saskatchewan, near its mouth, and trees of fair size are reported to occur on the island in Lake Winnipeg opposite the mouth of this river, and again on the south side of Long Point, in the same neighbourhood. I have not seen these cedars myself, but they are described as belonging to this species. The locality just mentioned would, therefore, constitute an outlying patch, removed 190 miles to the north-westward of the north-western point of the main area occupied by this tree.

Willow.—What appear to be three distinct species of willows, two of which, however, can only be considered as shrubs, extend northward beyond the mouth of the Churchill River, and are the most northern species of deciduous wood.

Balsam Poplar ("Rough-barked Poplar," "Cotton Tree," "Balm of Gilead," &c).—On the west side of Hudson's Bay this is the most northern species of poplar. It is abundant around York Factory, and attains a fair size along the lower part of the Nelson River. In descending the Great Churchill it becomes smaller and scarcer until the mouth of the river is reached, where it is rare.

Aspen (Trembling-leafed Poplar).—This tree, which is so abundant and of such a thrifty growth around the southern part of James' Bay and on the border of the prairie regions of the North-west Territories, does not extend quite as far north as York Factory. In ascending the Nelson River it was not met with until within a few miles of the Lowest Limestone Rapid. It extends northward nearly to the junction of the Little with the Great Churchill River.

White Birch (Canoe Birch).—This species terminates on Hayes' River, a few miles below the Steel River. On the Nelson, the first tree was met with at seven miles before coming to the Lowest Limestone Rapid, or at seventy from Point of Marsh. In descending the Little Churchill it disappeared about midway between the Recluse Lakes and the mouth, and in ascending the Great Churchill, it disappeared at eighteen miles above the forks. Along the Burntwood River and the upper part of the Nelson it is large enough for building canoes, but becomes better for this purpose to the northwestward, and is said to be very good around Lake Athabasca.

Rowan (Mountain Ash).—Common along the east side of Lake Winnipeg, and it is seen here and there along the Nelson River as far as White Mud Falls, where it disappears. Mr. Cochrane met with it on Island Lake.

Pigeon Cherry.—Found around Island and God's lakes, and northward to Knee Lake. On the Nelson it extends to a point some miles below

Sipi-wesk Lake, and on the Grass River to the junction of the west branch at Burnt Lake.

Forest Preservation.

Up to 1878 the great region covered by this report had been annually devastated by forest fires, ranging over large areas and destroying the timber in different localities from time to time, until, perhaps, more than half of it is already swept away. In that year I made a point of calling the attention of the Indian chiefs and head men to this great waste, and informed them that it was the wish of the Government that the timber (which the Indians had not before considered of any value) should not be thus destroyed, and requested them to make their temporary fires on the beach or on bare rock, and to extinguish their camp-fires in all cases before leaving. This they all promised to attend to, and the result has been that during 1879 no forest fires, as far as I could learn or observe myself, had occurred. The saving thus effected is worth to the country many times more than the cost of our explorations.

APPENDIX I.

—

ON SOME SILURIAN AND DEVONIAN FOSSILS FROM MANITOBA AND THE VALLEYS OF THE NELSON AND CHURCHILL RIVERS, FOR THE MOST PART COLLECTED BY DR. R. BELL IN THE SUMMER OF 1879.

BY J. F. WHITEAVES.

1. FROM THE BANKS OF THE RED RIVER, IN THE PARISH OF ST. ANDREWS, MANITOBA.

Receptaculites Oweni, Hall. (=*Coscinopora sulcata*, D. D. Owen, non Goldfuss.) A fine specimen, which, when perfect, was probably at least one foot in diameter. The occurrence of this species at Lower Fort Garry (which is in the parish of St. Andrews) was first placed upon record by D. Dale Owen in 1852, on page 181 of his "Report on a Geological Survey of Wisconsin, Iowa and Minnesota." According to Professors Hall and Whitney ("Geology of Wisconsin, 1862," vol I., p. 429) *R. Oweni* "is the common and abundant species of the Lead region and the one known as the 'lead-coral,' from its constant association with the lead-bearing rock."

Favosites prolificus, Billings. A characteristic fragment. This species, which was originally described from the Hudson River group of Anticosti, occurs also, as will be shewn further on, in rocks of the same age at Stony Mountain, Manitoba.

Halysites catenularia, Linn. One good specimen.

Monticulipora (Monotrypa), Sp. Indt. A fragment of a rather large, hemisphærical, or possibly sphœroidal coral, apparently allied to *Monotrypa undulata* Nicholson, but too imperfect to allow the whole of its specific characters to be ascertained. To the naked eye the specimen appears as a portion of a hemisphærical crust, about three-quarters of an inch thick in the thickest part and half an inch in the thinnest. The convex and presumably upper surface is almost covered with small,

4

irregular, but mostly annular, siliceous concretions, and the concave face looks as if it had been broken from a much thicker mass. When viewed with a lens the coral is seen to be made up of minute, polygonal, thin-walled, contiguous and continuous corallites, of different sizes, apparently arranged in groups. The larger corallites are about one-sixth of a line in diameter, and the smaller from one-eighth to one-tenth of a line. The cells are entirely filled with mineral matter, and the shape and position of the tabulæ cannot be satisfactorily defined.

Zaphrentis, Nov. sp.   Two imperfect specimens of an apparently undescribed species of *Zaphrentis* or *Streptelasma.*

Actinoceras Lyoni, Stokes.   The types of *A. Lyoni* are from Igloolik and Ooglit, in Arctic America, but Dr. Bigsby, on page 170 of the " Thesaurus Siluricus," gives Fort Garry as one of the localities of this species.   *A. Richardsoni* of Stokes, from Lake Winnipeg, may be the same shell in a different state of preservation, for, according to Stokes' descriptions, the only difference between *A. Lyoni* and *A. Richardsoni* is that in the former· " a small tube is seen within the siphuncle, but no radii have been traced from it," while in the latter the tube is said to be small and " surrounded by numerous laminæ or plates filling up the siphuncle." In Stokes' figures, however, the siphuncle of *A. Lyoni* is represented as larger in proportion to the size of the shell than it is in *A. Richardsoni.*   In the extremely large size of their siphuncle and in the apparently entire absence of any radii proceeding from the central tube, which latter cannot be discerned at all in some individuals, the two specimens collected by Dr. Bell at this locality, and several others from Stone Fort, Manitoba, in the collection of the Survey, agree much better with the descriptions and figures of *A. Lyoni* than with those of *A. Richardsoni.*

Illænus, Sp. (allied to and possibly identical with *I. latidorsatus*, Hall). An imperfect cast of a small *Illænus*, most likely the same as the trilobite from Fort Garry referred by D. D. Owen to *I. crassicauda*, Wahlenberg.   The specimen collected by Dr. Bell is, however, clearly not the true *I. crassicauda*, for in the original figure of that species in the "Petrificata Telluris Succanæ" (pl. 2, figs. 5 and 6) the central lobe of each of the ten body rings is represented as equal to about one-third of the entire diameter, whereas in the specimen from St. Andrews the central lobes of the body segments are equal to nearly three-fourths of their greatest diameter. The *Illanus* from this locality is too imperfect for the species to be identified with much certainty, but if not actually identical with *I. latidorsatus*, it appears to be very closely allied to it.

2. FROM LIMESTONE RAPIDS 100 MILES UP THE NELSON RIVER.

Leptæna sericea, Sowerby. Not uncommon.

Strophomena tenuistriata, Hall. One specimen. According to Davidson, *S. tenuistriata*, Hall, is merely a variety of *S. rhomboidalis*, Wilckins.

Strophomena filitexta, Hall. Several detached valves.

Strophomena subtenta, Conrad. A single valve.

Rhynchonella Anticostiensis? Billings. Two imperfect, badly preserved and small examples of a species of *Rhynchonella*, apparently identical with some larger and more perfect casts from the south-west shores of Lake Winnipeg, in the collection of the Survey, which have been identified by the writer with the *R. Anticostiensis*.

Murchisonia bellicincta, Hall. (=*M. major*, Hall.) A single large cast, which corresponds fairly well with the figures and description of this species.

Asaphus megistos? Locke. A cast of the pygidium only.

3. FROM "FIRST BIRCH BROOK," NELSON RIVER.

Strophomena alternata, Conrad. One valve.

Ecculiomphalus, Nov. sp. A single specimen.

4. FROM THE SECOND AND THIRD LIMESTONE RAPIDS OF THE NELSON RIVER.

Receptaculites Oweni, Hall. Several fragments.

Halysites catenularia, Linnæus. According to Dr. Bell this well-known species is quite common at this locality.

Eridophyllum, Nov. sp. A single fragment. The same species was collected by Dr. Bell at Fort Churchill, but in loose pieces of rock, and there is a fine specimen of it in the Museum of the Survey, from Stone Fort, Manitoba.

Strophomena alternata, Conrad.   One specimen.

Murchisonia bellicincta, Hall.   (=M. major.)   A large cast, precisely similar to one from the locality last mentioned.

Maclurea (near *M. Bigsbyi*, Hall).   Two tolerably perfect casts of a shell which may be an extreme variety of *M Bigsbyi*, but the outer whorl is wider above, and more obliquely compressed below, between the periphery and the umbilical margin, than the corresponding parts of the shell of *M Bigsbyi* are.   In a figure of the latter species recently published by Prof. Whitfield, the aperture is represented as a little higher than wide, whereas in the most perfect of the two Maclureas collected by Dr. Bell at this locality the maximum width of the aperture is about one-third greater than its height.

Endoceras (Cameroceras) annulatum? Hall.   Three distorted and imperfect examples of an *Endoceras*, which agree in most respects with the definition of *E. annulatum*.   The outline of their transverse section is rather oval than circular, but this circumstance may be due to lateral compression.

Oncoceras, Nov. sp.   One fine but somewhat distorted specimen.

5. From the Junction of the Little and Great Churchill Rivers.

Zaphrentis, Nov. sp.   Two specimens, one of which is the same as those from St. Andrews, previously mentioned.

Columnopora cribriformis, Nicholson.   A small but well-preserved example.

6. From Fort Churchill.   (Loose.)

Eridophyllum, Nov. sp.   Identical apparently with that from the Second and Third Rapids of the Nelson.

Rhynchonella capax, Conrad.   One very imperfect specimen.

Actinoceras Lyoni? Stokes.   A fragment of a siphuncle, consisting of a cast of four of the chambers.

The fossils from localities Nos. 1, 2, 3 and 4 are from limestones or dolomites which evidently belong to the same geological horizon.   On stratigraphical as well as on palæontological grounds there is good reason for supposing that these rocks represent the upper part of the Trenton Limestone, and that they are the equivalents of the Galena Limestone of Wisconsin and Illinois.   At Stony Mountain, Manitoba, they are immediately and conformably overlaid by true Hudson River rocks.

The few fossils collected on the banks of the Churchill, from localities Nos. 5 and 6, are insufficient to establish the exact age of the rocks in which they occur, but it is probable that both are referable either to the top of the Trenton Limestone or to the lower part of the Hudson River group.

7. FROM STONY MOUNTAIN, MANITOBA.

In 1875 Mr. R. W. Ells made an interesting collection of fossils from this locality, on behalf of the Survey, which has not hitherto been reported on. Stony Mountain, it may be mentioned, is a hill some fifty feet in height, on the western bank of the Red River, not far from Fort Garry. The species obtained by Mr. Ells are as follows:—

Chætetes delicatulus, Nicholson. Two specimens.

Monticulipora, Sp. One good example. This is the common Trenton and Hudson River species which Mr. Billings identified with *Stenopora fibrosa*, Goldfuss. It is also the coral figured by Prof. Hall on Plate 24, figures 1 g, h, i. (cœt. excl.) of the first volume of the Palæontology of New York, as one of the forms of *Chætetes lycoperdon*, Say. Dr. H. A. Nicholson places the coral represented in these figures among the synonyms of *Chætetes Fletcheri*, Edwards and Haime. In *C. Fletcheri*, however, the corallites are said to be rounded or oval, with comparatively thick walls, whereas in the present species the corallites are clearly polygonal, with thin walls.

Monticulipora (Diplotrypa) Whiteavesii? Nicholson. Two small specimens growing on the shells of brachiopoda.

Favosites prolificus, Billings. A fine large specimen, identified and labelled by Mr. Billings himself.

Streptelasma corniculum, Hall. Several well-preserved examples of a rather small *Streptelasma*, with a well-developed and smooth epitheca, precisely similar to the small individuals of *S. cornicula* figured by Rominger. These Stony Mountain *Streptelasmæ* represent the Hudson River group coral commonly referred to *S. corniculum*, rather than the typical form of that species from the Trenton Limestone.

Crinoidal Stems. Detached joints only.

Ptilodictya (Stictopora) acuta, Hall. A few characteristic fragments.

Strophomena nitens, Billings. Eight perfect examples of an entirely smooth form of this species.

Strophomena Hecuba, Billings. One dorsal valve.

Orthis testudinaria, Dalman. Abundant.

Orthis subquadrata, Hall. Many perfect and well-preserved specimens of an unusually coarsely ribbed variety of this shell.

Rhynchonella capax, Conrad. Several large and perfect examples.

Murchisonia gracilis? Hall. One small cast.

Cyrtolites ornatus? Conrad. One imperfect cast.

Ascoceras Newberryi, Billings. Two specimens.

The collection made by Mr. Ells at this locality shows, first, that a large portion of the mass of Stony Mountain consists of limestones, with clayey partings, which are identical, both in their lithological and palæontological characters, with the well-known rocks of the Hudson River or Cincinnati group of Southern Ohio and elsewhere; and, secondly, that these Hudson River rocks of Stony Mountain overlie, immediately and conformably, the buff-coloured, fossiliferous and more or less magnesian limestones of the Red River valley, which have already been assumed to be the representatives of the upper part of the Trenton limestone.

At Stony Mountain Dr. Bell also made a small collection of fossils, consisting of the following species.

Orthis testudinaria, Dalman.

Orthis subquadrata, Hall.

Rhynchonella capax, Conrad.

Cheirurus Icarus, Billings. One pygidium.

Calymene Blumenbachii, Billings, as of Brongniart. An imperfect pygidium. This is the common *Calymene* of the Trenton and Hudson River groups, identified by Billings and Dr. Nicholson with the *C. Blumenbachii* of Europe. Mr. S. A. Miller, however, says that the true *C. Blumenbachii* has not been found in North America, and that the species mistaken for it is the *C. senaria* of Conrad, which latter is a synonym of *C. calliteles,* Green.

A few fossils were collected by Dr. Bell at various places on the Churchill and Nelson Rivers, which appear to be of newer age than the Lower Silurian, but which are insufficient to indicate with much probability the exact geological horizon of the rocks in which they were found. The following are the localities at which these fossils were collected, with notes on the species,

8. THREE MILES EAST OF CHURCHILL RIVER.

Pentamerus (Sp. Undt.) Three casts of the ventral valve of a rather finely-ribbed *Pentamerus* in some respects like *P. occidentalis* Hall, from the Guelph limestone of Elora and Hespeler, Ont.

9. GILLAM'S ISLAND, NELSON RIVER.

Atrypa reticularis, Linnæus. Two specimens. Upper Silurian or Devonian.

10. WALKER'S ISLAND, OXFORD LAKE.

Atrypa reticularis, Linnæus. Five detached specimens, four with very fine ribs and one with remarkably coarse ones. Matrix a pale brick-red colour, just like that from the last locality.

11. YORK FACTORY. (LOOSE.)

Cyathophyllum Davidsoni, Milne-Edwards. (=*Acervularia profunda*, Hall.) One characteristic but much worn specimen.

Favosites (Sp. Indt.) A small rolled and rounded mass, of a species with small corallites.

The fossils from the last mentioned locality are certainly Devonian, but they may have been drifted from some distance.

c

APPENDIX II.

—

LIST OF PLANTS COLLECTED BY DR. R. BELL AROUND THE SHORES OF HUDSON'S BAY AND ALONG THE CHURCHILL AND NELSON RIVERS IN 1877 AND 1879.

The specimens have been kindly determined by Prof. John Macoun, F.L.S., Albert University, Belleville.

I. East coast of Hudson's Bay.

II. Churchill River.

III. North end of Lake Winnipeg.

IV. Nelson River between Lake Winnipeg and the coast of Hudson's Bay.

A. Plants crossing the Arctic Circle.

CATALOGUE.

Nos.		I.	II.	III.	IV.	A.
	RANUNCULACEÆ.					
1	Anemone parviflora, Michx	•				•
2	" multifida, D C.	•			•	•
3	" Pennsylvanica, Linn		•			•
4	Thalictrum dioicum, Linn				•	
5	" Cornuti, Linn		•			
6	Ranunculus aquatilis, var. trichophyllus				•	•
7	" multifidus, Pursh	•				•
8	" acris, Linn.	•				•
9	" Cymbalaria		•			•
10	" sceleratus, Linn	•				•
11	" flammula, var. reptans, Gr	•	•			•
12	Caltha palustris	•				•
13	Actœa spicata, var. rubra Gr	•				
	NYMPHÆACEÆ.					
14	Nuphar luteum, Smith (leaf only)	•				
	FUMARIACEÆ.					
15	Corydalis aurea, Willd				•	
16	" glauca, Pursh			•	•	

CATALOGUE—Continued.

Nos.		I.	II.	III.	IV.	A.
	CRUCIFERÆ.					
17	Nasturtium palustre, D C............		*		*	*
18	Cardamine hirsuta, Linn.............. ...				*	*
19	" pratensis, Linn................	*				*
20	Arabis Drummondii, Gr......................				*	*
21	Erysimum cheiranthoides, Linn............				*	*
22	Sisymbrium sophioides, Fischer............					
23	Draba incana, Linn......................		*		*	*
	VIOLACEÆ.					
24	Viola cucullata, Ait......................				*	*
25	" canina, var. sylvestris...............				*	*
*	CISTACEÆ.					
26	Hudsonia tomentosa, Nutt....,.............				*	
	DROSERACEÆ.					
27	Drosera rotundifolia, Linn.................				*	*
	CARYOPHYLLACEÆ.					
28	Lychnis apetala, Linn.....................		*			*
29	Arenaria lateriflora, Linn..................				*	*
30	" peploides, Linn		*			*
31	Stellaria longipes, Goldie..................				*	*
32	Cerastium arvense, Linn...................				*	*
33	" alpinum, Linn..................		*			*
34	Sagina nodosa, Frengl.....................				*	*	*
	GERANIACEÆ.					
35	Geranium Carolinianum, Linn..............				*	*
	POLYGALACEÆ.					
36	Polygala Seneca, Linn......		*		*	*
	LEGUMINOSÆ.					
37	Astragalus Canadensis, Linn				*	
38	" hypoglottis, Ker...............		*		*	*
39	" alpinus, Linn..................			*		*	*
40	" frigidus, Gray				*	*
41	" adsurgens, Pall...............				*	*
42	Glycyrrhiza lepidota, Nutt.................				*	
43	Hedysarum Mackenzii, Richard.............		*			*
44	Vicia Americana, Muhl....................				*	*
45	Lathyrus maritimus, Bigel.................		*		*	*
46	" ochroleucus, Hook				*	*
47	" palustris, Linn................., ...				*	

CATALOGUE—Continued.

Nos.		I.	II.	III.	IV.	A.
	ROSACEÆ.					
48	Prunus Pennsylvanica, Linn................				•	
49	Dryas integrifolia, Vahl..................	•	•			•
50	Geum rivale, Linn....				•	
51	" strictum, Ait				•	•
52	Fragaria Virginiana, Ehrh................				•	
53	Potentilla Norvegica, Linn................				•	▼
54	" Anserina, Linn..................				•	•	•
55	" fruticosa, Linn..................	•			•	•
56	" tridentata, Ait				•	▲
57	" palustris, Scop			•		•	•
58	" Pennsylvanica, Linn.............			•		•
59	" nivea, Linn.............			•			▼
60	" arguta, Pursh			•			•
61	" flabelliformis, Nutt..............			•			
62	Rubus Chamæmorus, Linn.................			•			▼
63	" triflorus, Richard			•			•
64	" arcticus, Linn....................	•	•			•
65	" strigosus, Michx..................			•		
66	Rosa blanda, Ait........................			•		₵	•
67	Amelanchier Canadensis, var. oblongifolia, Gray			•	•	•
68	Pyrus sambucifolia, Ch. & Schl			•		•
	SAXIFRAGACEÆ.					
69	Ribes prostratum, L'Her..................			•		•
70	" rubrum, Linn......................			•			•
71	" oxycanthoides, Linn...........			•			•
72	Parnassia palustris, Linu			•			•
73	Saxifraga aizoides, Linn	•			•	•
74	" Hirculus, Linn. ?			•			•
75	" tricuspidata, Retz			•		•
76	Heuchera hispida, Pursh..................			•	•	•
77	Mitella nuda, Linn......................			•		•
	HALORAGEÆ.					
78	Hippuris vulgaris, Linn................			•		•
79	Myriophyllum spicatum, Linn.............. ..			•		•
	ONAGRACEÆ.					
80	Epilobium angustifolium, Linn..............			•	•	•
81	" latifolium, Linn................			•			•
82	" coloratum, Muhl.............			•		•
83	Œnothera biennis, Linn...................			•		•
	UMBELLIFERÆ.					
84	Heracleum lanatum, Michx................			•		
85	Cicuta virosa, Linn			•			▼
86	Sium lineare, Michx			•		
	ARALIACEÆ.					
87	Aralia hispida, Michx................,.....					•

Nos.		I.	II.	III.	IV.	A.
	CORNACEÆ.					
88	Cornus Canadensis, Linn.................			•		•.-
89	" stolonifera, Michx................			•	•	•
	CAPRIFOLIACEÆ.					
90	Linnœa borealis, Gronov.................				•,	•
91	Lonicera involucrata, Banks		•			
92	Viburnum pauciflorum, Pylaie............				•	
	RUBIACEÆ.					
93	Galium trifidum, Linn...................				•	•
94	" boreale, Linn				•	•
	COMPOSITÆ.					
95	Nardosmia palmata, Hook................		•			•
96	" sagittata, Benth................		•			
97	Aster graminifolius, Torr. & Gr............		•			
98	" æstivus, Ait.....................				•	
99	" multiflorus, Linn................				•	•
100	Erigeron Canadense, Linn		.		•	
101	" Philadelphicum, Linn............		•			•
102	Solidago lanceolata, Ait				•	
103	" Canadensis, Linn...............				•	
104	Achillœa millefolium, Linn...............			•		•
105	Leucanthemum arcticum, D C.............		•			•
106	Artemisia Canadensis, Michx.............				•	
107	" biennis, Willd................				.•	•
108	" vulgaris, Linn.................				•	•
109	Antennaria dioica, Gærtn................				•	•
110	" plantaginifolia, R. Br...........			•		
111	Senecio palustris, Hook		•	•		•
• 112	" ——?				•	
113	" aureus, L., var. obovatus..........				•	
114	Arnica foliosa........................		•			
115	Hieracium Canadense, Michx.............				•	
116	Taraxacum palustre, D C................				•	•
	LOBELIACEÆ.					
117	Lobelia Kalmii, Linn			•		
	CAMPANULACEÆ.					
118	Campanula rotundifolia, Linn............			•	•	•
	ERICACEÆ.					
119	Vaccinium cæspitosum, Michx............	•				
120	" oxycoccus, Linn..............			•		•
121	" Vitis-Idæa, Linn.............		•		•	•
122	" Canadense, Kalm				•	•
123	" uliginosum, Linn.............	•	•			•

Nos.		I.	II.	III.	IV.	A.
124	Arctostaphylos uva-ursi, Spreng				•	•
125	" alpina, Spreng		•			•
126	Andromeda polifolia, Linn ....:........	•	•			•
127	Cassandra calyculata, Don		•			
128	Kalmia glauca, Ait	•	•			•
129	Ledum palustre, Linn	•	•		•	•
130	" latifolium, Ait...................		•			•
131	Pyrola minor, Linn....................				•	
132	" secunda, Linn.....................				•	•
133	" rotundifolia, Linn...................				•	•
	PLANTAGINACEÆ.					
134	Plantago major, var. Asiatica, Decaisne.......				•	•
	PRIMULACEÆ.					
135	Primula farinosa, Linn		•			
136	" Mistassinica, Michx		•			
137	Trientalis Americana, Pursh			•		
138	Lysimachia ciliata, Linn..................					
139	" thyrsiflora, Linn	•	•	•		
	LENTIBULIACEÆ.					
140	Utricularia vulgaris, Linn		•			•
141	Pinguicula vulgaris, Linn..................		•	•		•
	SCROPHULARIACEÆ.					
142	Veronica peregrina, Linn...................				•	
143	Castilleia pallida, Kunth...................		•			•
144	Euphrasia officinalis, Linn.....................			•	•	•
145	Rhinanthus Crista-galli, Linn.........				•	•
146	Pedicularis euphrasioides, Steph		•			•
147	" hirsuta, Linn ?.................		•			•
	LABIATÆ.					
148	Mentha Canadensis, Linn....................		•	•		•
149	Dracocephalum parviflorum, Nutt............		•			•
150	Scutellaria galericulata, L		•		•	
151	Stachys palustris, Linn....................		•	•		•
	BORRAGINACEÆ.					
152	Mertensia paniculata, Don		•		•	
153	" maritima, Don		•			
	GENTIANACEÆ.					
154	Gentiana Amarella, var. stricta....		•		•	•
155	Pleurogyne Carinthiaca, Griesb. var. pusilla, Gr.		•			•
156	Menyanthes trifoliata, Linn..................		•			•

CATALOGUE—Continued.

Nos.		I.	II.	III.	IV.	A.
	CHENOPODIACEÆ.					
157	Chenopodium album, Linn				•	•
158	" glaucum, Linn		•			
	POLYGONACEÆ.					
159	Polygonum aviculare, Linn		•		•	•
160	" amphibium, Linn		•		•	
161	" cilinode, Michx				•	
162	" viviparum, Linn	•	•			•
163	" lapathifolium, Ait		•		•	•
164	Rumex maritimus, Linn					
165	" salicifolius, Weinn			•		•
	ELÆAGNACEÆ.					
166	Elæagnus argentea, Pursh			•	•	•
167	Shepherdia Canadensis, Nutt		•		•	•
	SANTALACEÆ.					
168	Comandra umbellata, Nutt			•		
	EMPETRACEÆ.					
169	Empetrum nigrum, Linn	•	•			•
	URTICACEÆ.					
170	Urtica gracilis, Ait		•		•	
	BETULACEÆ.					
171	Betula glandulosa, Michx			•		•
172	Alnus incana, Willd				•	•
	SALICACEÆ.					
173	Salix candida, Willd			•		
174	" myrtilloides, Linn		•		•	•
175	" vestita, Pursh		•	•		
176	" ——?		•	•		
177	" ——?			•		
	CONIFERÆ.					
178	Juniperus communis, Linn				•	•
179	" Sabina, var. procumbens	•			•	
	TYPHACEÆ.					
180	Sparganium simplex, Huds				•	•
181	" minimum, Bauhin		•			•

CATALOGUE—Continued.

Nos.		I.	II.	III.	IV.	A.
	NAIADACEÆ.					
182	Potamogeton lucens, L.				*	
183	" rufescens,Schrad				*	*
184	" pectinatus, Linn				*	
185	" perfoliatus, Linn				*	
	ALISMACEÆ.					
186	Triglochin maritimum, Linn				*	*
	ORCBIDACEÆ.					
187	Habenaria rotundifolia, Richard		*			
188	" hyperborea, Lindl				*	*
189	Spiranthes Romanzoviana, Cham		*		*	
190	Corallorhiza innata, R. Br		*			*
191	Cypripedium guttatum, Swartz ?		*			*
	IRIDACEÆ.					
192	Sisyrinchium Bermudianum, Linn				*	*
	LILIACEÆ.					
193	Smilacina trifolia, Desf.		*			
194	" bifolia, Ker				*	*
195	" stellata, Desf.				*	
196	Lilium Philadelphicum, Linn					*
197	Tofieldia palustris, Huds		*			
	JUNCACEÆ.					
198	Luzula parviflora, var. melanocarpa Gray	*				*
199	Juncus alpinus, var. insignis Fries				*	
200	" Balticus, Dethard				*	*
201	" tenuis, Willd				*	
	CYPERACEÆ.					
202	Eleocharis palustris, R Br				*	*
203	Scirpus atrovirens, Muhl				*	
204	" validus, Vahl				*	
205	Eriophorum gracile, Roth		*			
206	Carex aristata, R. Br.?					*
207	" aurea, Nutt				*	
208	" canescens, Linn		*			*
209	" gynocrates, Wormsk		*		*	
210	" scoparia, Schk				*	
211	" straminea, Schk				*	
212	" stricta, Lam				*	
213	" vesicaria, Linn		*			*
214	" vulpinoidea, Michx				*	

CATALOGUE—Continued.

Nos.	GRAMINEÆ.	I.	II.	III.	IV.	A.
215	Alopecurus aristulatus, Michx	•				
216	Calamagrostis Langsdorffii, Trin........	•		•	•	
217	Agrostis scabra, Willd.....................				•	
218	Glyceria fluitans, R. Br				•	•
219	Poa alpina, Linn	•				•
220	" serotina, Ebrh................				•	
221	" laxa, Hænke				•	
222	Festuca ovina, Linn				•	•
223	Elymus dasystachyum				•	
224	Hordeum jubatum, Linn..				•	•
225	Beckmannia crucæformis, Hook............		•			
	EQUISETACEÆ.					
226	Equisetum sylvaticum, Linn...............		•			
227	" limosum, Linn		•		•	
	FILICES.					
228	Polypodium vulgare, Linn.................				•	
229	Asplenium Trichomanes, Linn..............	•				
230	Aspidium fragrans, Swartz.................	•				
231	" spinulosum, Swartz..............					
	var. dilatatum, Gr................			•	•	
232	Cystopteris fragilis, Bernh		•		•	
233	Woodsia Ilvensis, R. Br....................				•	
234	Botrychium Lunaria, Swartz		•			
	LYCOPODIACEÆ.					
235	Lycopodium clavatum, Linn...		•			
	MUSCI.					
236	Sphagnum subsecundum, Nees					•
237	Polytrichum strictum, Hook					•

APPENDIX III.

—

LIST OF FRESH-WATER MOLLUSCA FROM MANITOBA AND THE VALLEY OF THE NELSON RIVER.

The following list includes some species collected in Manitoba, which Mr. Whiteaves, of the Geological Survey, has kindly determined.

LAMELLIBRANCHIATA.

1. *Unio rectus*, Lamarck. Red River, Manitoba.

2. *Hyridella* (?) *radiata*, Lamarck. Numerous in Lake Winnipeg and the Nelson River.

3. *Hyridella luteola*, Lamarck. (=*Unio siliquoideus*, Barnes.) Red River, Manitoba.

4. *Lampsilis flavus*, Rafinesque. (=*Unio rubiginosus*, Lea.) Red River, Manitoba.

5. *Theliderma quadrulus*, Rafinesque. (=*Unio lachrymosus*, Lea.) Red River, Manitoba.

6. *Dysnomia plicata*, Lesueur. Red River, Manitoba.

7. *Metaptera alatus*, Say. Red River, Manitoba.

8. *Complanaria complanata*, Barnes. Common in the Nelson River, but larger and finer in the Red and Assiniboine Rivers.

9. *Strophitus Pennsylvanicus*, Lamarck. (=*Anodonta undulata*, Say.) Lake Winnipeg and Great Playgreen Lake.

10. *Anodonta* (Sp. uncertain.) Red River at Winnipeg.
    Nos. 4, 5 and 6 are characteristic Western species.

11. *Sphœrium transversum*, Say. ⎫ Both found in numbers in the
    ⎪ stomachs of sturgeon caught in
12. *Sphœrium striatinum*, Lamarck. ⎭ Great Playgreen Lake.

GASTEROPODA.

13. *Valvata* (*Tropidina*) *tricarinata*, Say. Found in the stomachs of sturgeon·caught in Great Playgreen Lake.
5

14. *Limnæa stagnalis*, Linné.   Lake Winnipeg, Nelson River and lakes and rivers to the south-eastward.

15. *Linnophysa catascopium*, Say.   Great Playgreen Lake.

16. *Physa heterostropha*, Say.   Inhabits the same waters as *Limnæa stagnalis*.

17. *Bulinus hypnorum*, Linné.   Ponds in Manitoba.

18. *Helisoma trivolvis*, Say.   Around Winnipeg and in Manitoba.

19. *Helisoma bicarinatus*, Say.   Lake Winnipeg.

20. *Segmentina armigera*, Say.   Abundant in Great Playgreen Lake.

APPENDIX IV.

—

LIST OF LEPIDOPTERA FROM THE NELSON AND CHURCHILL RIVERS AND THE WEST COAST OF HUDSON'S BAY.

Herr Geffcken of La Tour de Peilz, Switzerland, has kindly supplied the following list of the Lepidoptera of the region explored. The specimens were collected by the Venerable Archdeacon Kirby (now of London, England), who laboured for many years in this and other parts of the Northwest Territory.

1. Papilio Turnus, Linn.
2. . " Zolicaon, Boisd.
3. Colias Christina, Edw.
4. " Chippewa, Ed.
5. " Nastes, Boisd. Churchill.
6. " *Nov. sp.* Allied to C. Hecla and C. Boothii, but distinct from both. Found at Churchill or north of York Factory.
7. Danais Archippus, Fab.
8. Argynnis Triclaris, Hub.
9. " Frigga, Thunb, *var.* Laga.
10. " Atlantis, Edw.
11. " Freya, Thunb.
12. " Chariclea, Schneid.
13. Melitæa Tharos, Drury.
14. Vanessa Milberti, Godt.
15. " Hunter, Drury.
16. " Cardui, Linn,
17. " Atalanta, Linn.
18. " Antiopa, Linn.
19. Limenitis Arthemis, Drury.
20. Erebia Discoidalis, Kirby. York Factory.
21. " Fasciata, Butler. North to Churchill.
22. " *Nov. sp.* North Churchill.

23. Satyrus Nephele, Kirby.
24. Chionobas Jutta, Hubn.   York Factory.
25. Polyommatus Xanthoides ?   Boisd.
26. Macroglossa Flavofasciata ?
27. Alypia Maccullochi ?   Kirby.
28. Telea Polyphemus, Linn. } Evidently south of York Factory.
29. Platarctia Parthenos,Fab. }

APPENDIX V.

—

LIST OF COLEOPTERA COLLECTED BY DR. R. BELL IN 1879 ON THE NELSON AND CHURCHILL RIVERS.

The species of Coleoptera collected during my exploration of the Nelson and Churchill rivers have been kindly determined by Dr. J. L. LeConte of Philadelphia, who has forwarded the following list of them.

1. Carabus tædatus, Fabr.
2. Nebria Sahlbergi, Fisch.
3. Calathus ingratus, Dej.
4. Platynus ruficornis, Lec.
5. Pterostichus orinonum, Leach.
6. " empetricola, Dej.
7. Amara hæmatopus, Dej. (=Stereocerus similis, Kirby & Lirus lacustris, Lec.)
8. Dytiscus confluens, Say.
9. " anxius, Mann.
10. Gaurodytes lutosus, Crotch.
11. Gyrinus (immature and undeterminable).
12. Lathrobium simile, Lec.
13. Silpha Lapponica, Linn.
14. " trituberculata, Kirby.
15. Coccinella 12-maculata, (=incarnata, Kirby,=picta, Randall.)
16. Hippodamia quinque signata, Kirby.
17. Buprestis Nuttalli, Kirby.
18. Melanophila Drummondi, Kirby.
19. Chrysobothris trinervia, Kirby.
20. Photinus (Ellychnia) corruscus. (small var.)
21. Podabrus, allied to piniphilus.
22. Telephorus fraxini, Say.

23. Criocephalus agrestis, Kirby.
24. Xylotrechus undulatus, Say.
25. Acmæops pratensis, Laich. (=strigilata, Fab.)
26. Leptura subargentata, Kirby.
27.   "   sex-maculata, Linn.
28.   "   chrysocoma, Kirby.
29. Monohammus scutellatus, Say.
30. Pogonocherus mixtus, Hald.
31. Orsodachna Childreni, Kirby.
32. Odoxus vitis, Linn.
33. Chrysomela spireæ, Say.
34. Gonioctena arctica, Mann.
35. Graptodera bimarginata, Say. (=Pliciponnis, Mann,=vitivora,
                Thomas.)
36. Stenotrachelus arctatus, Say.
37. Meloe Americanus, Leach.(=angusticollis, Lec.)
38. Lepyrus colon, Linn.

APPENDIX VI.

—

LIST OF BIRDS FROM THE REGION BETWEEN NORWAY HOUSE AND FORTS CHURCHILL AND YORK.

The following is a list of the birds, of which either the skins or the eggs were actually obtained, in the region between Norway House and Forts Churchill and York. Many other species were noted, and a list of these is reserved to be verified and enlarged the coming season. I am indebted to Mr. H. G. Vennor, of the Geological Survey, and Mr. P. Kuetzing, naturalist and taxidermist, for assisting in the determination of the skins. Several of these were given to me by Dr. Percy Mathews and Mr. Henry Johnstone, of York Factory.

1. *Haliætus leucocephalus,* Bald eagle. Rather scarce.
2. *Pandion haliætus,* Briss. ; Osprey, or Fishing eagle. Common. Several nests seen along the Churchill and Grass rivers.
3. *Falco communis,* Gm. ; Peregrine or Duck hawk, male. York Factory.
4. " *columbarius,* Linn. ; Pigeon hawk. Norway House to Fort Churchill.
5. " *sparverius,* Linn. ; male. York Factory.
6. " *sacer,* Forst. ; Ger-falcon. York Factory. A fine specimen, presented by Mr. Fortescue.
7. *Buteo borealis,* Gm. ; Red-tailed hawk. Fort Churchill.
8. *Brachyotus palustris,* Bechst. ; Swamp owl. Fort Churchill and York Factory.
9. *Nyctea nivea,* Daudin ; Snowy owl. Abundant throughout the district in winter.
10. *Surnia ulula,* var. *Hudsonica,* Gm. ; Hawk owl. Fort Churchill and York Factory.
11. *Corvus Americanus,* Aud. ; Common crow. On Lake Winnipeg the young were able to fly in the beginning of July. Not often seen in the woods. Common on Hudson's Bay.
12. " *corax,* Linn. ; Raven, or Barking crow. Breeds throughout the district.

13. *Ceryle Alcyon,* Linn.; King-fisher. Lake Winnipeg to York Factory. Rare towards Fort Churchill.

14. *Colaptes auratus,* Linn.; Yellow-shafted woodpecker. Very numerous, owing to the abundance of food afforded by the extensive *brulés.* The Hairy Woodpecker is also very common.

15. *Collurio borealis,* Vieil.; Great northern shrike. York Factory.

16. *Loxia leucoptera,* Gm.; American cross-bill. A specimen, which flew on board ship in Hudson's Strait, was presented by Dr. Mathews.

17. *Quiscalus purpureus,* Bartr.; Purple blackbird. York Factory.

18. *Scolecophagus ferrugineus,* Gm.; male, Rusty Grakle. York Factory.

19. *Melospiza melodia,* Wils.; Song-sparrow. Norway House.

20. *Dendrœca œstiva,* male, Gm.; Yellow-poll warbler. York Factory.

21. *Eremophila alpestris,* Forst.; Shore lark. Fort Churchill and York Factory.

22. *Plectrophanes nivalis,* Linn.; Snow Bunting. York Factory.

23. *Turdus migratorius,* Linn.; American Robin. Common throughout the district.

24. *Tachycincta bicolor,* Vieil.; White-bellied swallow. York Factory.

25. *Chordeiles Virginianus,* Gm.; (western variety) Night hawk. York Factory. Common southward. The Whip-poor-will was not seen nor heard north of Norway House.

26. *Lagopus albus,* Gmel.; Willow ptarmigan. Abundant at Churchill and York in winter, and comes as far south as Norway House.

27. *Bonasa umbellus,* Linn.; Ruffed grouse. Rare as far north as York Factory.

28.   "   *Canadensis,* Linn.; Canada grouse. Rare at Fort Churchill.

29. *Pediœcetes phasianellus,* Linn.; Pin-tailed grouse. Some of these birds were shot near Dog's Head, Lake Winnipeg. Thence I have found them eastward as far as Long Lake and Pic River on Lake Superior.

30. *Strepsilas interpres,* Linn.; Turnstone. York Factory.

31. *Grus Canadensis,* Linn.; Sand-hill crane. Norway House.

32. *Botaurus minor,* Gm.; Little bittern. York Factory.

33. *Gambetta flavipes,* Gm.; Yellow-shanks. Common throughout the district.

34. *Gambetta melanoleuca*, Gmel.; Tell Tale: Stone Snipe. Norway House.

35. *Tringoides macularius*, Linn.; Spotted sandpiper. Norway House to York Factory.

36. *Numenius borealis*, Forst.; Eskimo curlew. Abundant in July and August at Fort Churchill, as were also the Hudsonian Curlew, Golden Plover, and other species of which no specimens were brought home.

37. *Aegialitis semipalmata*, Wilson. Semipalmated Sandpiper. York Factory.

38. *Larus argentatus*, Brunn; Herring gull. Fort Churchill.

39. *Sterna hirundo* (?), Auct.; Black-headed tern. Very common in the larger lakes and on the shores of Hudson's Bay.

40. *Erismatura rubida*, Wils. Ruddy Duck. York Factory.

41. *Anas boschas*, Linn.; Grey or Stock duck, or Mallard. This is the commonest duck in the district. Breeds in considerable numbers along the Nelson and Little Churchill Rivers.

42. *Dafila acuta*, Linn.; Pintail duck. Breeds near Norway House.

43. *Bucephala clangula*, Linn.; Common Golden-eye or "Tree Duck." Also breeds near Norway House.

44. *Spatula clypeata*, Linn.; Spoon-bill duck. On Lake Winnipeg the young were nearly full-grown in the beginning of July.

45. *Querquedula Carolinensis*, Gm.; Green-winged teal. Very common near Norway House; scarce northward.

46. *Mergus cucullatus*, Linn.; Hooded merganser. Young going south in flocks on the Nelson River in September.

47. " *merganser*, Linn.; Red-headed merganser. Common throughout the district.

48. *Pelionetta perspicillata*, Linn. Surf Duck. York Factory.

49. *Anser Canadensis*, Linn.; Canada goose. Breeds in considerable numbers along the Churchill River. Most of the young could fly in the beginning of August.

50. " *hyperboreus*, Pal., var. *albatus*; Lesser snow-goose. One specimen which had been shot at Fort Churchill was presented by Mr. J. R. Spencer. Is very rare on the west side of Hudson's Bay.

51. *Anser hyperboreus*, Pal.; Common White wavy. Abundant at Churchill and York during the spring and autumn migrations.

c

52. *Cygnus Americanus*, Sharpless; Whistling swan. A few are shot
    every spring at Fort Churchill, from which place a speci-
    men was presented by Mr. J. R. Spencer.

53. *Pelecanus fuscus*, Linn.; Brown pelican. Breeds in the smaller
    lakes near Lake Winnipeg and north-westward. Several
    specimens were shot in Lake Winnipeg in October.

54. *Colymbus septentrionalis*, Linn.; Red-throated diver. York Factory.
    Mr. Ross has shot a specimen flying past at Norway
    House.

55.   "   *torquatus*, Brunn; Great Northern diver. Breeds in many
    lakes throughout the district. Mr. Fortescue informed me
    that in the spring of 1878, just after the ice broke up at
    York Factory, great numbers of these birds congregated
    in the mouth of Hayes' River, a circumstance which had
    never been observed in any previous season.

The Passenger Pigeon was seen in small flocks in the upper part of
the Nelson River in the beginning of September, 1878. It very rarely
passes York Factory, and has never been known at Fort Churchill.
The common American Snipe was met with near the Nelson River
above Split Lake. I saw one specimen of the Woodcock at York
Factory in the end of August last. This bird is not uncommon in
Manitoba, although the fact is not generally known. The Pine
Grosbeak was frequently seen on the Churchill River in the end of
July, showing that it probably breeds in this region.

APPENDIX VII.

VARIATION OF THE COMPASS.

The following list shows the variation of the compass in twenty-one localities in the territory explored during the season. The observations were taken with as much care as was possible while making such a rapid survey of an extensive region, where one had to attend, unaided, to such a variety of different matters. The local attraction, which exists in many places, especially among the Laurentian and Huronian rocks, sometimes renders it difficult to ascertain the true variation for any locality. Sir Henry Lefroy (who visited this region in 1843-44), in a letter which I have received from him on this subject, says :—" I used a new 7-inch compass, and used it carefully, but the results differ much more than I can account for. This is particularly the case where a change of geological formation occurs—say, for example, about the narrows of Lake Winnipeg—and I should be greatly interested in a good comparison by means of A.M. and P.M. sights on the 'Dog's Head' and the 'Bull's Head,' and on the opposite side to both. * * About Oxford Lake I have 12° 58', 10° 11', 14° 21', in near proximity." Among other causes influencing the variation in this region, besides that of change in geological formation on a large scale, above alluded to, I have noticed beds of magnetic iron, deposits of iron sand, dykes of diorite, great magnetic boulders, sudden change in the general level in passing from one region to another, proximity of a cliff or bank or even of a thick grove. or (when very close) a single large tree.

	Variation E.
1. Little Churchill River, 24 miles south of its junction with the Great Churchill. (The north side of the " forks " being in lat. 57° 30' 57.34" and about long. 95° 30')	11° 30'
2. Little Churchill River, 5 miles north of last	10° 30'
3. At the north side of the junction of the Little with the Great Churchill River, in the above latitude	12° 30'
4. Great Churchill River, 22 miles north of the above junction ..	15° 00'
5. Great Churchill River, 27 miles from its mouth	6° 30'
6. Fort Churchill, on the west side of the river, 4 or 5 miles from its mouth. (Lat. 58° 44' 43.04")	11° 00'

7. York Factory, S. W. side of the fort. (In 1878 I found only about 5° 30′ at the N. E. side, but there appears to be some local attraction there).....................................   7°   00′

8. Hill River, about 20 miles above its junction with Fox River (1878)...   9° 45′

9. Nelson River, 63 miles from Point of Marsh, or the N. E. extremity of Beacon Point.............................   8° 45′

10. Nelson River, First (or lowest) Limestone Rapid, (lat. 56° 36′ 6.″), about 77 miles in a straight line from Point of Marsh..   11° 30′

11. Nelson River, Broad Rapid, 23 miles S. W. of last..........   11° 30′

12. Nelson River, outlet of Split Lake. (Lat. 56° 16′ 27″)......   18° 00′

13. Grass River, outlet of Witchai ("Stinking") Lake, about 12 miles S. W. of the upper end of Split Lake, or about lat. 56°..   16° 30′

14. Nelson River, north side of outlet of Sipi-wesk Lake, at south end of Cross Portage. (Lat. 55° 13′ 29.38″).............   16° 30′

15. Nelson River, Chute at outlet of Duck Lake (Duck Portage)..   19° 15′

16. Nelson River, 12 miles below White Mud Falls. (Lat. 54° 45′ 48.14″)......................................   14° 30′

17. Nelson River, Western Channel of East River, 5 miles south of Pipestone Lake....................................   16° 30′

18. Nelson River, Junction of Pine River with East River, 6 miles above Sea River Falls................................   16° 00′

19. Norway House..   14° 00′

20. Point at east end of Mossy Point (at outlet of Lake Winnipeg), about one mile north of Warren's Landing..............   16° 45′

21. Lake Winnipeg, north side of Poplar Point, near extremity..   15° 15′

I am indebted to Sir J. H. Lefroy, of London, for the following "memorandum of observations of variation on Lake Winnipeg in 1843-44."

	Variation E.
1. Fort Alexander..	13° 56′
2. Grassy Narrows.......................................	14° 14′
3. Opposite Bull's Head..................................	16° 18′
4. Opposite Dog's Head..................................	15° 24′
5. By Beren's River.....................................	16° 55′
6. Point near Wesleyan Mission..........................	14° 26′
7. By Mossy Point.......................................	19° 23′
8. A little beyond (lat. 52° 29′).........................	15° 27′
9. Norway House..	15° 13′
10. Second Rocky Point..................................	17° 03′

The following were taken in 1877 in connection with the Dominion Lands Department:—

Mouth of Poplar River, east side Lake Winnipeg ....   15° 20′ E.

Black River, north of Winnipeg River........................   13° 00′ E.

www.ingramcontent.com/pod-product-compliance
Lightning Source LLC
Chambersburg PA
CBHW021417090426
42742CB00009B/1167